VERSE FROM PUSHKIN
AND OTHERS

VERSE
FROM PUSHKIN
AND OTHERS

BY

OLIVER ELTON

GREENWOOD PRESS, PUBLISHERS
WESTPORT, CONNECTICUT

Originally published in 1935
by Edward Arnold & Company, London

First Greenwood Reprinting 1971

Library of Congress Catalogue Card Number 72-114517

SBN 8371-4822-7

Printed in the United States of America

CONTENTS

	Page
INTRODUCTION	7

PUSHKIN

From RUSLAN AND LYUDMILA	27
From POLTAVA	48
From EVGENY ONEGIN	50
TALE OF THE TSAR SALTAN	78
TALE OF THE DEAD PRINCESS AND THE SEVEN CHAMPIONS	109
TALE OF THE GOLDEN COCK	127
TALE OF THE POPE AND OF HIS WORKMAN BALDÀ	135
TALE OF THE FISHERMAN AND THE LITTLE FISH .	142
'When in the warm springtime'	149
THE BRONZE HORSEMAN	152
THE WINTER ROAD	168
TO THE BROWNIE	170

NEKRASOV

THE BIRTHPLACE	171

TYUCHEV

'The snow still whitens on the lea'	174

ALEXANDER BLOK

'My spirit is old'	175
'Dim grow the edges of the river'	176
'*Life*, our bark, has stranded'	177

Contents

	Page
'Pipes on the bridge struck up to play'	178
'With tears and merriment and pain'	179
'Here in the dusk, as winter fled'	180
'What long-forgotten gleam is this?'	181
RAVENNA	182

ANNA AKHMATOVA

THE WOUNDED CRANE	184
INDEX	185

INTRODUCTION

I

The Russian novel has long been open to the English reader; but with Russian poetry he is much less familiar. It is not, in the same measure as the novel, an international possession; and it offers, like all poetry, special discouragements to the translator. There are indeed some admirable versions, to which I shall refer; but unhappily our own poets have been slow to take up the task. As for the experiments in the present volume, I only hope that they may draw some readers to the Russian. It would be much, too, if (in Dryden's phrase) they were to 'appear of a passable beauty when the original Muse is absent'; and more, if they could aid in correcting any false impression that has been left by the Russian novel.

For is not many a well-read and well-disposed Englishman repelled by the Russian novel as much as he is attracted? Those who know the Russian world, past or present, at first-hand will be proof against mistakes. But the novel often presents an alien and even a sinister scene. It throws into relief either the darker and more turbid side of the racial character, or its more ineffectual and helpless side. Probably Dostoevsky, more than all the rest, has to answer for this presentment; such is his force, and such his profundity—a sham profundity though it often be. But he is not alone: the comedy of Gogol has its uncanny side; the heroes of Turgenev, from Rudin onwards, fail to cheer us; and over many a tale of Chekhov hangs a blight, or palsy. For relief, we turn to Chekhov's other tales, or to his letters with their gaiety and sanity and faith in science. The stories of a writer like Andreev,

Introduction

and much of the post-revolutionary fiction that is now being translated, will deepen the gloom. There must be truth in this picture, for the witnesses are too many to question; it reflects the long historic tragedy of Russia; and yet it is easy to see it all out of scale. The later books of Tolstoy cast their shadow back upon the earlier; reading *The Kreutzer Sonata* or *Resurrection* we too soon forget Kitty and Levin, and Natasha, and *The Cossacks*. We forget, that is, the *poetic* soul and genius of the race, which is so quickly smothered in satire, in propaganda, in religiosity; all at the cost of simple human feeling, and of permanent art. And the soul and genius of the race are best seen in the poetry itself. Here, in their fullest expression, are found the spirit of lightness and gaiety, the love and perception of nature, and the purity of religious passion; and here, above all, is unadulterated art. Russian lyric is a storehouse of these treasures. But to hear 'the original Muse,' in her widest range of tones, the Russians still go back to Pushkin.

Those tones, indeed, are often melancholy and troubled. The lines that I have translated from Nekrasov and from Blok are only stray examples. Pushkin himself can be deeply melancholy; but it is a sane and virile melancholy. His *Bronze Horseman* has the note of tragic grandeur. Yet these are not his prevailing moods, and he is faithful to every mood; being, like his contemporary Leopardi, an artist born and vowed; more of an artist, from the first, than any of our own 'romantic poets' of the same period. The Russians can never say enough of his many-sided plastic skill. Some of his best verse, such as his folk-tales, is almost impersonal: it is pure, disinterested, classic art, obeying only its own law. No political changes seem to impair the cult of Pushkin. His manuscripts are cherished and minutely studied. There are large learned editions,

Introduction

and cheap ones with a scholarly text;[1] and there is an ever-increasing literature, with which I do not pretend to cope. We have, too, his delightful letters; his life, his loves, have been scrutinized, for such is the doom of poets; we know as much about him as we do about Byron or Shelley. A bare note on his career will make plainer the sequence of the present translations.

II

Alexander Sergeevich Pushkin, born in Moscow on May 25 (O.S.), 1799, came of a family of the higher gentry, patrician in its tastes and limitations, and in its culture French. From his mother's grandfather he inherited, not without some pride, a streak of hot Abyssinian blood. While a schoolboy at the Lyceum of Tsarskoe Selo he studied the prose and verse of the *grand siècle*, and of Voltaire; also the elegant amorous rhymes of Evariste Parny (1753–1814). He was to be influenced by André Chénier; and much of his precision and lightness

---

[1] The text I have used is that of B. Tomashevsky and K. Khalabaev in one volume (sixth edition, Moscow-Leningrad, 1930). The huge miscellany (hereafter referred to as *Works*) edited by S. A. Vengerov (six volumes, SPB., 1907–15) yields—after digging—matter of much value, especially in the notes of N. O. Lerner. The literature is summarized in the masterly sketch by Prince D. S. Mirsky (*Pushkin*, 1926), who is the best and most learned guide, for English readers, over the whole field. See his short *Modern Russian Literature* (1925); *History of Russian Literature* (down to 1881; 1927); *Russian Literature, 1881–1925* (1926); and his notes to *The Oxford Book of Russian Verse* (1924), chosen by the Hon. Maurice Baring. Mr. Baring's introduction, like his *Outline of Russian Literature*, is the work of a poet and translator in natural sympathy with the Russian genius.

Introduction

of hand may be ascribed to his French reading. These qualities are seen in his adolescent lyrics, and still more in his first long poem, *Ruslan and Lyudmila*, published in 1820. For three years (1817–20) Pushkin ran wild in St. Petersburg; and his life, up to the date of his marriage, was, like Byron's, often irregular. But, like Byron, he wrote none the less and none the worse and often all the better for his distractions. He had many amours and some loves and many disenchantments, and everything found expression. In 1820, for some rash political verses, he was deported to the South of Russia; and he was now able, though under supervision, to travel widely. His talent flowered afresh; he roamed in the Caucasus and the Crimea, and with the gypsies in Bessarabia. *The Prisoner of the Caucasus*, *The Gypsies*, and other romantic tales show the influence of Byron's lays in their energy and their exotic colouring. But Pushkin could not fall into Byron's laxity of craftsmanship. From the greater Byron, the poet of *Beppo* and *Don Juan*, he was to profit in *Evgeny Onegin*.

Still incautious, and regarded askance by the authorities, he was placed for two years (1824–6) in a kind of internment at his parents' home in Mikhaylovskoe, in the province of Pskov. Here he mixed with the common people freely, read and wrote incessantly, continued to produce beautiful and impassioned lyrics, studied Shakespeare, and worked at his historical tragedy *Boris Godunov*. In 1825 came the death of Alexander I and the December revolution, in which many of Pushkin's friends were involved. Nicholas I forgave his political sympathies and brought him to Moscow. He was allowed to write, though the censorship of the monarch and his agents was an oppressive burden. Pushkin brought with him part of the great rhymed novel *Evgeny Onegin*, which took him eight years

Introduction

(1823-31) to complete. In 1828 he wrote the heroic and romantic *Poltava*, which marks his advance towards a severer style. His wanderings between Petersburg and Moscow, his second trip to the Caucasus, and his troubled last years were all most fruitful. But his short dramas like *The Stone Guest* (who is Don Juan's Commander), and his prose tales like *The Queen of Spades* and *The Snowstorm*—all miniature masterpieces—do not concern this volume. Pushkin poured out lyrics to the end, but after 1826 devoted himself more and more to prose. In verse, his great performances were now the *skazki* or folktales, and *The Bronze Horseman*. In 1831 he married the beautiful Nathalie Goncharova, much younger than himself: 'a bright papilionaceous creature,' as Carlyle would have called her, given to flirting, intent on shining in the big world, and without any understanding of Pushkin's mind or aims. She is described however as a faithful and not undutiful wife. Pushkin, vext by debts and by the snubs of the censor, was also inflamed by jealousies, one of which proved fatal. He was forced, or so he thought, into a duel with Baron George D'Anthès; and died of his wound on January 29, 1837.

III

Pushkin speaks of *Ruslan and Lyudmila* as 'light rubbish,' and as 'a playful tale,' founded on old-time legends. On these, and not on French literature only, he had been nourished from his childhood, like Walter Scott. Some he learned from popular chapbooks; some, it is uncertain how much, from his nurse Arina Rodionovna. But the old stories also reached him in a more sophisticated form through contemporary verse, as embroidered by Zhukov-

Introduction

sky, Karamzin and others. *Ruslan* was but the greatest example of a current fashion, eclipsing all the rest. The 'sources' have been explored, and an origin either popular or literary has been found for almost every name and incident in the poem.[1] Yet the result is entirely Pushkin's own. The story is most ingeniously tessellated, and the episodes all enhance the impression of unity. The arguments inserted in the translation will make the construction plain. There is a streak of Voltairian irony that does not go too well with the simpler roguish humour of the folk-stories; and Pushkin still keeps his schoolboy taste for parody and extravaganza. But there is also a spray of pure poetry, like that which besprinkles Lyudmila from the waterfall. The *Prologue* is an afterthought and appeared first in the edition of 1828; many of its wonders are absent in the poem. The air-borne wizard is there, but not the cat of letters or the thirty champions. These beings, familiar to folklore, forecast the *skazki* of ten years later: poems far more thoroughly harmonized and finished than *Ruslan*. But already can be seen Pushkin's easy stream of narrative, and his beautiful directness and simplicity.

IV

I have included some lines from *Poltava*, as a prelude to the portrait of Peter the Great in *The Bronze Horseman*. *Poltava*, though full of magnificent passages, is wanting in unity, being half military epic and half Byronic romance. From *Evgeny Onegin* I have given long extracts, laced together by a sketch of the plot. As Pushkin

[1] For facts as to dates, sources, etc., see M. Khalansky in *Works*, i. 572–90.

Introduction

tells us, its form is suggested by that of Byron's *Don Juan*. The story strays into all manner of excursions, descriptions and personal confidences. Behind this *genre* lies the old Italian 'romantic epic'—of which the master is Ariosto—with its mixture of poetry, satire, and magic. The mood may change from verse to verse, from line to line; the favourite device is a sudden cooling of the temperature, a drop into mockery at the end of the stanza. The likenesses between Pushkin's poem and Byron's mighty miscellany are somewhat delusive. There are, indeed, the amours, the world-weariness, and the *blasés* satirical comments; but these belong to Onegin rather than to the author. The canvas, naturally, is narrower than that of Byron, who ranges over the South and the Near East and England. A deeper difference lies in the quality of the writing. Byron's, often so admirable, is often merely slapdash. Pushkin is like a consummate skater, flying ahead, or circling beautifully, with never a motion wasted. The story of *Onegin* may not seem strong enough to bear the weight of some five thousand lines; but its simplicity prints it on the mind, and it holds the bright, loose fabric together. The hero, though a poor creature, retains our attention. He is drawn, and drawn by a master; we are not asked to like him, only to believe in him. All is in keeping: his dandyism, his boredom, his priggery, his wicked caprice in provoking the duel, and his punishment; there is the justice of poetical comedy. Tatyana holds our love and sympathy throughout. The poet does not elaborate her transformation from a passionate *ingénue* into a great lady. Yet, as we read, the change seems natural; and, after all, Tatyana she remains. She still loves Onegin, although she sees through him; and she keeps her marriage vow. Her letter is one of the great letters of fiction, and her dream one of the great dreams. In this

Introduction

poem, as everywhere, Pushkin is a master of landscape, and especially of winter landscape; we hear the sleigh-bells, we feel the brush of the snowflake on our faces. The stanza, somewhat intricate, lends itself to every change of pace and modulation. Pushkin's papers show how diligently he wrought at his text; one chapter, describing Onegin's wanderings after the duel, was finally banished to a supplement.

V

Much of the attraction of *Onegin* is independent of the story; but Pushkin's true goal, in respect of structure, was the story, just as his goal, in respect of form, was an ever greater strictness and simplicity. The *skazki* or folk-tales, written during the years 1831–3, mark a clear stage in this double progress and a new perfection in Pushkin's art; they show not only his style and music but his 'shaping spirit of imagination,' all at their height; and they have long since taken their rank as classics. They are not 'fairy tales,' for they contain no fairies. They are built upon old popular themes and stories. The events that decide the issue and impel the action are magical. The actors may be human beings, with or without preternatural powers; or they may be animals, or demons. But all have human motives and passions and behave logically in their own world. The moral, if any, is not preached, it is unfolded by the incidents. The good prosper in the end, the wicked or presumptuous weave, unawares, their own discomfiture. They may be knocked on the head, or banged about, or forgiven when they have become harmless. It is, again, the justice of comedy, and Pushkin observes it serenely, without emphasis.

Introduction

We have his definition of the term *popular*:

> Any nation you will has a mode of thinking and feeling, a mass of customs, inherited beliefs, and usages, which belong to it exclusively. Climate, mode of living, and belief give to each nation a particular physiognomy, which is more or less reflected in its poetry.

These words apply above all to folklore; and in the course of years Pushkin gathered a mass of popular tales, verses, proverbs, jests, and customs. The story [1] of his gleanings is a long one. It is thought that during his stay at Mikhaylovskoe he had drawn on the stores of Arina Rodionovna for some of his material. Now, in the spring of 1831, he was at Tsarskoe Selo in the company of Gogol, and also of Vasili Andreevich Zhukovsky, sixteen years his senior. Zhukovsky, then the *doyen* of Russian poetry, was a lyrist, a reformer and master of versecraft; he was also a mighty translator from English and German, who had opened new horizons in literature to his fellow countrymen. The two friends now sat down in amiable rivalry, to compose each a *skazka*. Zhukovsky's *Tale of the Tsar Berenda*, in hexameters, is lively and interesting, but commonplace by the side of Pushkin's *Tale of the Tsar Saltan*. This was published in the same year, 1831; and the poet has left several memoranda which show his rough material. His method here is the familiar one of the snowball: the marvels accumulate. Every new one is re-told, more than once, by different speakers. Moreover, it is ironically prophesied, as it would seem at haphazard, by the wicked women who wish to delay the happy reunion of Saltan with his wife and son. But the irony is two-edged; for behold, it

[1] See the detailed study by N. N. Trubitsyn in *Works*, iv. 52–72.

Introduction

is just these marvels that come true and crown his happiness. The poem ends, in the conventional fashion, upon the note of drink: '*I*,' says the poet, 'drank beer, drank mead,' at the final feast. Pushkin's aim is to turn into finished works of art tales that had long been on the lips of the people, purging them of crudities and shunning the vices of the imitators. *Saltan* extends to nearly a thousand lines, but it does not seem long, for in the dream we lose count of time. It is perhaps the most satisfying, in its flawless evolution and its harmony of tone, of all Pushkin's folk-poems.

The Tale of the Golden Cock, or Cockerel, is much shorter, and in temper sharper, and in movement swifter. The cock is a sardonic bird who will stand no nonsense. The astrologer-eunuch and the princess of Shamakhan have been thought to import a somewhat exotic, non-popular element. The story is familiar from the operatic adaptation by Rimsky-Korsakov to many who know not Pushkin's verse. The censor, as usual, was on the watch, and pounced upon the line 'Govern, lying on thy side' as an improper apostrophe to a tsar.[1]

The Tale of the Dead Princess and the Seven Champions was written in 1833. Maidens hunted by their stepdames and dying, in appearance, for a season, only to revive and to be wedded happily, are common in German and Russian folklore. Pushkin imparts an elegance and a chivalry of his own to these stock incidents. The bearing of the princess and of the seven brothers is gallantly conceived; and the call of Elisey to the sun and moon and wind is perhaps the summit, poetically speaking, of all these folk-tales. *The Dead Princess* is not such a per-

---

[1] See Lerner in *Works*, vi. 467; and the same writer on *Saltan*, vi. 412–15; on *The Dead Princess*, vi. 454–5; on *Baldá*, vi. 418–19; on *The Fisher*, vi. 444–5.

Introduction

fect whole as *Saltan*; the story straggles in comparison, though it is braced together by the invocations of the step-mother to her mirror. Editors have amused themselves by quoting from a letter of Pushkin's to his wife: 'Hast thou looked in the glass, and been convinced that with *thy* face there is nothing in the world to compare?'

The Tale of the Pope and of his Workman Baldà, finished in 1831, was not printed in the poet's lifetime. Indeed, he foresaw the frown of the censor over the epithet of 'porridge-head,' or as we should say pudding-head, applied to a cleric. Zhukovsky, to avoid trouble when he published the poem in 1840, turned the pope, or parish priest, into a merchant; and it appears that the pope was not restored to the seat of mockery until the edition of 1882. Pushkin has left his notes of the story; it is on the common theme of the *strong servant* who performs difficult and sometimes preternatural tasks for a comic wage that is at last exacted. The admirable rough-and-tumble of the business is echoed in the metre, or no-metre. This is rhymed, in rough lines of varying length; it has been described as 'hewn prose'; but the English ear will hardly accept it, and I have substituted a free kind of *Ingoldsby* verse.

The Tale of the Fisherman and the Little Fish is on another common topic; a boon is granted to a benefactor by a supernatural person, or animal, who abuses his privilege and at last is no better off than when he began. The fishwife eggs on her man till her terms are unbearable and the golden fish vanishes in disgust. Pushkin by his repeated formulæ gives a pleasing mock-epical turn to the tale, which is delicately balanced. Once more, the rhythm, which is derived from folk-verse, cannot be reproduced, and my version can barely suggest it, for it is neither

Introduction

regular metre nor yet free prose. The lines range from nine to eleven syllables; each begins and ends with a lighter syllable, and tends to fall into three groups of words, each bearing at least one accent: [1]

Have píty | O my físh | my príncess!

There are many more rhymes, and many varieties of length, in the fragment 'When in the warm springtime'; and here I use plain prose, since the long, caressing diminutives defy translation. These lines are, properly speaking, a fable, not a *skazka*. There is no magic; the beasts simply have human feelings, callings, and nicknames. There is much promise of fun in their parliament; but we get no further than the roll-call and do not know how Mrs. Bear was to be avenged.

VI

The Bronze Horseman was written in 1833, and published posthumously, in 1841. Here Pushkin has cut his story to the bone. He had originally intended to portray Evgeny at length, with his room and his books and his dream of a home with his Parasha; he was to be fair-haired and pock-marked. All this is dropt, and Evgeny becomes a type of humanity in its barest terms: an insignificant little civil servant, singular only in his fate. Still he is a person, a living sufferer; and he turns, at bay, upon the most powerful person in the world; for Peter, the man of bronze upon his bronze charger, is still that. Evgeny

---

[1] I have drawn here on the accounts of Mme. N. Jarintsov in her instructive introduction to *Russian Poets and Poems* (Oxford, 1917) and of V. Bryusov ('Pushkin's poetic technique,' in *Works*, vi. 362).

Introduction

defies him in two untranslatable words, *uzho tebe!*, 'Thou, look out!' They are, morally speaking, the climax of the poem; for they have, after all, been *said*; although the angry horseman seems to come to life, and chases Evgeny out of his poor wits. The poet holds the scales between these two personalities, the one immense, the other infinitesimal. Slowly they approach, and clash; then they separate, then clash again and at last part for ever. Peter is no longer the man of Poltava; he is now a natural force, a creator; and creation is not a merciful or moral process. He still remains on guard, while the Evgenys go under . . . So we may muse without end, as great art always permits. The Russian judges seem to agree that Pushkin's style is at its highest in this poem: entirely flexible, and homely or majestic as may be required. The measure follows the waves of living speech, and the lines are more freely broken than in his earlier verse. At the date of the flood (November 7, 1824) Pushkin was at Mikhaylovskoe, far from the scene. The story lay in his mind, and the poem was completed nine years later, after much revision. He mentions his chief authority, Berkh, in his prefatory note. There was also a story told, by an eye-witness, of a man who had been cut off by the waters and had saved himself by climbing upon one of the lion-figures; and yet another, of a strange dream that had haunted, in the year 1812, a certain major. In this dream the statue of Peter (which there was, in fact, a project of moving) had appeared to pass, clattering as it went, to the palace of Alexander, saying to him: 'Young man, to what hast thou brought my Russia? While I am in my place my city is not in danger.' Then the statue in the dream went back; and the real statue, in the end, was not displaced. The poem was much edited by the Emperor Nicholas, who disallowed allusions to the 'idol,' or 'image,'

Introduction

and to the 'dowager in purple'; and we are told that the true complete text was not printed during the nineteenth century.[1]

VII

A few translations from other poets, on whom it would be out of place to dwell here, have been added. Nikolay Alexeevich Nekrasov (1821–77) is represented only by the fierce little reminiscence entitled *The Birthplace*. Not one of the greater artists, he was one of the most powerful and widely honoured writers of his time; he reflects the sufferings, the manners, and the life of the Russian folk. His work of widest range, *Who lives happily in Russia?*, can be read in Mrs. Soskice's translation in 'The World's Classics.' I also give a few lines from the great lyrist Fedor Ivanovich Tyuchev (1803–73). Alexander Blok (1880–1921), the leading poet of later times, is best known in England by his splendid and portentous work called *The Twelve*. His earlier verse is of quite another stamp, and my examples reveal rather a spirit of Shelley's tribe. His lyrics have an elusive beauty, and often seem a web of pure sound and imagery, just held together by the logic of feeling. Yet the noble *Ravenna* will show how firm of outline, how distinct and Roman, Blok can be when he will. One piece by the living poetess, Anna Akhmatova, is appended. Her lyrics often present a passionate situation, and have been compared to Browning's; they are beautifully concise, and clear, like good medallions.

[1] Lerner, *Works*, vi. 448 ff.; and see the study by V. Bryusov, *Works*, iii. 456–72.

VIII

In these translations the original metres are preserved, in respect of the number of syllables in the line and of the rhyming system—with the following exceptions. (1) In the last three of the folk-poems, for reasons already offered. (2) *Ruslan* and *The Bronze Horseman*, in the Russian, are rhymed irregularly, though still not at random. The single and double rhymes are about equal in number; and the general principle, dear to the Russian ear, is to alternate, in couplets or in groups, the two species of ending. But the rule is that a given single (or double) rhyme shall not be *immediately* succeeded by a fresh single (or double) rhyme. Pushkin now and then neglects this rule at the beginning of a new paragraph. I have done so more frequently, although the English reader, accustomed to his *Marmion*, will hardly notice the practice, or be offended by it. (3) Subject to these requirements, I have not felt bound to follow the precise irregularities of the original, line by line.

Russian is highly inflected and abounds in double rhymes of great variety. In English, as we know, such rhymes are far more limited in kind and easily become heavy or monotonous or ludicrous. The translator must choose: shall he take the risk and keep them, or shall he drop them in the hope of making better verses? Some have dropt them, and have been well justified by the result. But in facing a poem of any length I have felt that to quit Pushkin's measure is really to quit the field. His rhythm is one of his glories, it is near to the heart of his work; and the translator, though he can never impart its secret, should at least try to respect its formula. I am encouraged in this belief by the success of an almost forgotten predecessor, who has been re-discovered by Prince

Introduction

Mirsky [1] and who handles the double rhymes with much skill. This is Thomas Budge Shaw (1813–62), Lector in English literature at the University of St. Petersburg and tutor of Russian grand dukes. He figures in the *D.N.B.*: and his *Outlines of English Literature* (1848, etc.) were long popular in this country. In *Blackwood's* (1845) are to be seen his three excellent articles on Pushkin, containing translations of many lyrics; they show poetic instinct, and are often very close.

If the reader can bear with this studio talk, there are three other important distinctions to be made. (1) In English, one of our richest resources in a disyllabic or 'iambic' measure is to introduce an allowance of rippling, or trisyllabic, feet. This is foreign to the classical Russian practice, and I have eschewed it. (2) But there is another deviation from the metrical 'base,' or pattern, which is equally foreign to Pushkin, but which is so native to our own verse that it cannot be wholly sacrificed. The classical Russian ('iambic') line is accented with far more regularity than ours. The accents indeed may be weightier or lighter, and the subtlety of the effect depends greatly upon such gradations. The 'pyrrhic,' or foot of two unaccented syllables (x x), is indeed abundant, though less so than in English verse; and Pushkin's management of such feet in *contiguous* lines is most delicate. The 'spondee' (′ ′), with two heavy accents, is rarer. The 'trochee' (′ x), with the accent displaced or 'inverted,' is much rarer still. Thus a line like

His éye was dímmed, | crámpt was | his breást,

though in a familiar English rhythm, is not in a Pushkinian rhythm. Still I have tried to be sparing of these effects,

[1] See his *Pushkin*, pp. 243–53, for examples.

Introduction

remembering how my best adviser has said to me that 'Pushkin in English ought to go like butter.'

(3) Lastly, in the synthetic Russian, as in Greek and Latin, *grammatical* inversion (quite a different thing from metrical inversion) is everywhere, and admits of every nice shade of emphasis. No doubt, in an English rendering, the less inversion there is, the better. For we associate it either with the manner of Milton (which is here to be shunned at all costs), or else with the looser manner of Scott ('Lord Marmion then his boon did ask'), which is unsound. It is a question how far to go in this matter, for almost all our poets use inversion more or less; and some critics may find that I have gone too far. These explanations, which are not excuses, will show some of the breakers ahead in the present venture; which may still have been worth while, if it leads some wise person to say to the reader, 'Why do you read this? Get to Pushkin himself. Look what someone[1] says about him, who really knows the language from within':

> He treated the language as a great orchestrator writes an orchestral score, and as a great conductor interprets the lights and shadows and renders the musical values of the score.

IX

Many of the poems in this volume have not, so far as I know, been translated into English before, or not in the original measures. There is an interesting but I fear neglected version of the whole of *Onegin* by Lieut.-Col.

---

[1] Maurice Baring, *Lost Lectures*, 1932, pp. 188–9; this paper on Pushkin contains some notable verse translations, above all one of *The Prophet* (also printed in *Slavonic Review* for July, 1933).

Introduction

Spalding (*Eugene Onéguine*, 1881); the stanza is retained (though not the double rhymes), and there are useful notes. Parts of *Saltan* and of *The Bronze Horseman* are given in English verse by Mme N. Jarintsov in her *Russian Poets and Poems* (Oxford, 1917). A few of her lines (and also of Col. Spalding's) I find to be identical with my own, which were hit on independently; but they are of an obvious kind, and could hardly have been different. Mme Jarintsov's other book, *The Russians and their Language* (Oxford, 1916), is also a good companion, and a lesson to all who seek English equivalents for the untranslatable. The valuable *Anthology of Russian Literature*, edited by Dr. Leo Wiener (two volumes, 1903), contains some excellent versions by various hands. I have also seen Mr. John Pollen's *Rhymes from the Russian* (1891) and his *Russian Songs and Lyrics* (1916); and Mr. C. E. Turner's *Translations from Pushkin* (1899), done for the birthday centenary); these are unrhymed, and include *The Bronze Horseman*. Mr. P. E. Matheson's elegant lyrical translations can be seen in his *Holy Russia and Other Poems* (1918).

Needless to say, there are many translations of note by my fellow-contributors to the *Slavonic Review*.

X

The following poems, here revised, have already appeared in that journal: *Ruslan and Lyudmila*,[1] with *Prologue*; Tatyana's portrait, letter, and dream, also the duel-scene, with a few other stanzas, from *Onegin*; *Saltan*, lines 1–350; *The Dead Princess, The Golden Cock, The Pope and Baldà, The Bronze Horseman, The Winter Road, The Brownie, Ravenna,* and *The Wounded Crane*.

Introduction

I thank the editors and publishers for their hospitalities, and for their ready permission to use all this material. To one of them, my friend Professor Sir Bernard Pares, K.B.E., the book owes a particular debt. He has seen the greater part of it, and his advice, both on points of accuracy and on points of form, has been generously given and is of the utmost value. Mr. Gleb Struve, of the School of Slavonic Studies in London University, has supplied some valuable corrections and has spared no trouble. Professor A. Bruce Boswell, of Liverpool University, has likewise reviewed many pages, greatly to their profit. Also I am obliged, for light thrown upon questions submitted to them, to Professor S. Konovalov, to Mr. Basil Slepchenko, and to Prince Mirsky. For 'faults escaped' of any kind, only the translator is responsible.

Further acknowledgments are due to the editor and publishers of the *London Mercury* for their courtesy in permitting the reprint of Nekrasov's *Birthplace*; and to the editor of the *News-Letter*, for the same service in respect of the lines of Tyuchev, and of Blok's poem 'With tears and merriment.'

The accentuation of Russian proper names is given in the Index.

O. E.

Oxford,
    December, 1934.

PUSHKIN

From RUSLAN AND LYUDMILA

Prologue

A chain hangs down with golden fetters
From a green oak-tree, in a bay,
And on that chain a cat of letters
Walks round for ever, night and day;
Goes singing, as she rightward ambles;
Turns leftward, and a tale relates.
Strange things are there: the wood-sprite rambles;
The water-maid in branches waits;
And there, on paths unnoted, thickens
The slot of beasts to man unknown;
A cottage there, on legs of chickens,
Unwindowed, doorless, stands alone.
With visions wood and vale are teeming;
And there at dawn, the tide comes streaming
On a deserted sandy verge,
And thirty chosen champions splendid,
By their sea-uncle still attended,
In turn from the bright wave emerge.
A prince is travelling by, and sweeping
Before them all a warrior brave
Away across the wood and wave;
There, served by a brown wolf and loyal,
In prison pines a lady royal.
Beside the Dame Yagà there stalks
A pestle: as on feet, it walks.

Sick king Kashchèy on gold is gloating;
There, the true Russian scent is floating!
—And there was I, and drank my mead,
And saw the leafy oak, and sat there
Down by the sea. The learned cat there
Told me her tales; and one, indeed,
Comes back to mind; I now disclose it,
And care not if the whole world knows it.

The Wedding

I tell you deeds of days gone by;
From far tradition comes the story:—

In thronging audience-chamber high
Vladimir,[1] like the sun in glory,
With friends and stout heirs held carouse,
His youngest daughter to espouse
To valiant Prince Ruslan; he swallowed
Mead in a ponderous bowl, and followed
With healths to them and all the house.

Our good forefathers dined at leisure;
The ladles, at their leisure too,
And wine in silver cups, full measure,
Went round, and beer in bubbling brew.
All hearts were flooded with enjoyment
As the foam fizzed upon the brim;
The bearers, in their grave employment,
Serving each guest, bowed low to him.

[1] Vladimir was Grand Prince of Kiev from 980 to 1015.

Ruslan and Lyudmila

But now the talk was all confounded
Into one buzz, by that gay ring;
When hark! a pleasing voice resounded
To the loud psaltery's flying string;
All hushed; and now were celebrated
By a melodious Bayan [1]
The marriage wreath, by Lel [2] created,
Charming Lyudmila, and Ruslan.

But he, enamoured, sick with yearning,
Ate not nor drank, with passion burning;
Watched his beloved sitting by,
And glowed, and heaved an angry sigh;
Bit his moustachios, while he reckoned
Impatiently each tardy second.

There, by the boisterous nuptial board,
With brows all glum, with never a word,
Sat three young champions dejected.
The ladles unreplenished stood
And the round goblets passed neglected.
They had no relish for their food;
Were downcast, discomposed and jealous,
Nor heeded soothsaying Bayan.
   Hid in their souls the poison ran
Of love and hate; these luckless fellows,
All three, were rivals of Ruslan.
One was Rogday, a dashing sworder,
Whose blade had shifted back the border

[1] A kind of Kievan Homer, who sang to a stringed instrument called 'gusli.'
[2] A god of love and marriage, in old Slavonic legend.

Of Kiev's rich and rolling plain;
The next, unrivalled as an eater,
But mid the clash of steel discreeter,
Farlaf, a brawler proud and vain;
The last, a man of fire and passion,
The young Khazarian[1] khan, Ratmir;
And all, in pale and sullen fashion,
Sate cheerless, over that good cheer.

    The feast is done; and in due muster
They rise, and shout, and throng and cluster;
All scan the youthful pair; the bride
Casts down her gaze, as one who wholly
Is out of heart and melancholy;
The bridegroom beams with joy and pride.

    But darkness all the world is wrapping;
The dead of night is nearly come;
The warriors, o'er the mead-cup napping,
Bow their farewells, and make for home.
Ruslan, in joy and exultation,
Caresses in imagination
The beauties of the bashful maid;
While the great duke, on both bestowing
The benediction that is owing,
Is full of sadness unbetrayed.

    And now the young Lyudmila, plighted,
Is taken to the marriage bed;
And now the evening lamp is lighted
By Lel; the fires are quencht and dead.

---

[1] The Khazars were the most settled and peaceful of the Asiatic neighbours of Kiev and Byzantium.

Ruslan and Lyudmila

Ruslan's dear hopes are nigh repayment;
Love's gifts are soon to make him glad;
And downward falls the jealous raiment
On woven carpets of Tsargrad.
Hear ye the passionate words low-spoken
And the sweet kisses? do ye hear
The interrupted murmurs broken,
The last shy plaint?   And now comes near
The moment, and the happy groom
Foreknows . . . when, suddenly, from under
A flashing cloud, a clap of thunder!
The lamp goes out, there whirls a fume,
And all is quaking, all is gloom;
Ruslan is faint with fear and wonder.
Twice, through a dreadful hush, there sounded
A stranger-voice; and Someone flew
Upward, with thickest smoke surrounded,
And murkier than the mist that blew.
The empty room once more is still;
The bridegroom rises, and in rivers
Cold sweat pours down his face; he shivers
In fear; his questing fingers chill
In the dumb dark have vainly sought her,
'My love is gone! ah, misery, where?'
The mirk is dense; she is not there;
Some power unknown away hath caught her.

[*Vladimir promises Lyudmila to the man who shall find her.   Ruslan and the three rivals ride off to seek her, but soon part company, and have sundry adventures.   Ruslan meets an old man, Fin, who after telling his own story informs him that the thief is the wizard Chernomor, but that he, Ruslan, shall win his wife in the end.   She is now in Chernomor's castle.*]

Lyudmila Captive

All night the young princess was laden
With deep oblivion, and fast
Locked in a dreadful dream; at last
With hot and troubled soul the maiden
Woke in dim terror; and she cast
Her mind again to thoughts of rapture,
Joyously hoping to recapture
Someone—but whom? 'Where is my dear,
My lord?' she murmurs; 'is he here?'
Then glances round, half-dead with fear.
Where, hapless lady, art thou banished?
Where has thy own dear chamber vanished?
—She lies on down, and overhead
By a proud canopy is shaded;
The curtains and the sumptuous bed
Are tassel-hung and costly-braided;
All round are precious webs, brocaded;
All round, like flames the jewels gleam;
The perfume rises in a steam
From golden censers:—but I need not
Describe a wizard's palace; no,
Scheherazade long ago
Forestalled me there, and I proceed not.
And yet a room, however bright,
Is joyless, with no friend in sight.

Three girls, all prodigies of beauty,
In lightsome and alluring dress,
Appear, and draw to the princess,
And bow to earth, to pay their duty.

Ruslan and Lyudmila

And then the first approaches, pacing
With noiseless step, and soon is lacing
In one gold tress Lyudmila's hair.
She plaits with fingers light as air,
—An art we know today—and winding
A coronal of pearls, is binding
Therewith the forehead pale and fair.
The next demurely down is gazing;
And now the graceful form is blazing,
Invested with a sarafan,
Magnificent, cerulean.
A veil like a transparent cloud
The youthful shoulders now doth shroud,
The bosom, and the yellow tresses
—A jealous garment that caresses
Charms worthy among gods to dwell!
A pair of sandals lightly presses
The feet—a perfect miracle.

And the third handmaid now is bringing
A girdle all bepearled; and near,
The voice of one unseen is singing
A song of happiness and cheer.
But ah! no necklet's jewelled treasure,
No flattering, gay, melodious voice,
No sarafan, no pearls, give pleasure
Or make Lyudmila's heart rejoice.
And vainly in the mirror shining
Are the fair form and gorgeous dress;
With eyes bent low and motionless
She speaks not, heartsick and repining.

Now all true lover-folk, the dark
Recesses of the heart perusing,

—I mean, their own—will surely mark
That when a weeping woman, musing
In sorrow, does not steal askance
Her wonted and judicious glance
Into the mirror, her affliction
No longer is a jest, or fiction.

   They leave her; now, alone again
And all perplexed, behold her straying
Up to the latticed window-pane,
With melancholy eye surveying
A dismal, endless, deathly plain.
Over the level land there stretches
A snowy carpet clear and bright;
Further, a range of summits reaches,
Sullen, monotonously white,
Asleep for ever, mute. No sight
Of cottage smoke or traveller going
Across the snows! no huntsman blowing
A cheery horn, whose echo fills
The desert of those empty hills!
At times a whistling wind flies sadly
O'er the bare plain, and riots madly,
And on the edge of the gray skies
The naked forest quivering lies.

   Lyudmila, desperate and tearful,
Just hid her face; the scene was fearful.
Alas!—but what was now in store?
She hurried to a silver door;
And it flew open to a sound
Of music, and Lyudmila found
She stood within a garden fairer,

More charming than Armida's, rarer
Than all the Taurid prince could own,
Or that great emperor, Solomon.
Before her rising now she sees
A noble coppice of oaktrees
That rustle in the wind and waver;
A row of myrtles of sweet savour;
A laurel thicket; by them nested
Gold oranges, and proudly-crested
Cedars, palm-alleys,—and all these
Glassed in the waters. Every copse,
The valleys, and the low hill-tops
Now feel the fires of spring renew them.
The meadow-lands enchanted stay
Under the sorcery of May,
Whose cool fresh airs are wafted through them.
The nightingale of China now
Trills on the shadowy, quivering bough;
The diamond spray from fountain flashes
And gaily to the heavens plashes;
The statues that below them gleam
Might be alive,—or do we dream?
And would not Phidias, fosterling
Of Pallas and of Phœbus, fling
His magic chisel in vexation
And gaze on these with admiration?
Here in a fiery pearly bow
The waterfalls come down and spatter
And on the marble edges shatter;
Here, in the woodland shade, below,
The sleepy streamlets hardly flow;
And, for a shelter cool and quiet,
Here, through the never-fading green,
Bright arbours glimmer, barely seen.

The paths breathe fragrance, with a riot
Of roses, in their living sheen.
But she, unseeing, only ponders,
And inconsolably she wanders.

[*Lyudmila is spirited back to her bed. Negroes enter, carrying a long beard, at the end of which is Chernomor; and while he wears it, nothing can subdue him. He also wears a magic cap. Lyudmila seizes him by the beard; he tumbles down and is removed, leaving the cap. (Ruslan, meantime, has been attacked by Rogday and has cast him into the water; where he is taken down by a water-sprite, or rusalka.) Lyudmila, trying on the cap before the glass, turns it wrong side forward, and becomes invisible and safe. Ruslan wanders on to*]

The Valley of the Dead

Now, as the morning clouds gleam bright,
A spacious valley comes in sight.
Against his will, our hero shivers;
Behold, an ancient battle-field
In a blank country! Here revealed,
Men's bones lie yellowing; and quivers,
Corslets, and many a rusted shield,
And harness, strew the mounds; the bone
Of a dead hand still clasps the sabre;
A tufted helmet, grass-o'ergrown,
Has an old rotting skull for neighbour;
A warrior's skeleton, complete,
With charger prostrate at his feet,
Lies moveless; arrows, too, and lances
Are pinned into the swampy ground,

Ruslan and Lyudmila

And peaceful ivy wraps them round,
And nothing ever comes, or chances
To vex that desert hush profound.
The sun, high up in heaven and bright,
On this Dead Vale pours down his light.

[*Musing on the chances of mortality, Ruslan picks up a helmet and armour; and a pike, for he finds no sword that is worthy of him.*]

Already the wide earth is sleeping;
The rose of sunset pales and dies;
Blue vaporous mists around are creeping;
A golden moon begins to rise.
And musing, as the steppe grows dimmer,
Ruslan rides down the darkening track,
And sees, beyond the night-fog's glimmer,
A monstrous hummock looming black.
—What fearful thing is yonder, snoring?
Ruslan comes close, and closer still,
And seems to hear, as he waits poring,
A breathing from that wondrous hill.
Calm and unfaltering is he,
While his horse trembles and stands pricking
Its ears in panic; jibbing, kicking,
Its head it tosses stubbornly,
And all its mane on end is sticking.

The hillock, in pale vapour shrouded,
Illumined by a moon unclouded,
Clears quickly; and a prodigy
Confronts the brave Ruslan (but see,
My words are pale, my colours dim!)
A living Head is facing him!

The two huge eyes are shut and sleeping;
And, as it snores, the plumes that curl
Upon the helmet waver, sweeping,
And there on the dark crest unfurl,
Like shades that pass and flit and whirl.
There, in its dreadful beauty lowering,
There, on the sullen steppe uptowering,
Guarding that nameless empty land,
Begirt with silence, doth it stand,
Vast, threatening, in its misty curtain,
Before the prince. And he, uncertain
In mind, is eager to dispel
That strange mysterious sleep, and seeking
To scrutinise the miracle,
Draws near the head, and never speaking
Rides round it, pauses at the nose,
Tickling the nostrils, as he goes,
With point of pike; and at the thrust
The eyes are opened in a twinkling,
The mouth yawns wide, the brows are wrinkling,
And the head—sneezes; and a dust
Flies up, and all the steppe is shaking;
A whirlwind rises in a gust;
A flight of owls comes whirring now
From eyelash and moustache and brow;
The silent thickets are awaking
And echo back the sneeze; and snorting,
The restive horse darts off, cavorting;
The warrior is all but flung.
A resonant voice behind him rung:
'Insensate warrior, whither questing?
Turn, shameless man! I am not jesting;
Or I will make one gulp of thee!'
Ruslan looked round, and scornfully

Reined in his steed as though to wait,
And only smiled in answer, proudly.
And the head frowned, and bellowed loudly,
'What wouldst thou have with me? what fate
Sends such a visitor, so late?
Listen: 'tis night, and I am minded
To have my sleep, and thou wilt find it
Best to begone; so, stay not here!'
When this rude language strikes the ear
Of our illustrious cavalier,
With dignity sore ruffled by it
He shouts, 'Thou empty sconce, be quiet!
I've heard a saying old and true,
"The forehead's big, the brains are few!"
So, touch me, if thou darest to!' [1]

And then, aflame and dumb with passion
And stifled spite and indignation,
The head blows out its cheeks; there flies
A sparkle from the bloodshot eyes;
The lips are quivering and foaming,
From mouth and ears a steam is coming;
And suddenly, with all its might,
It puffs a blast against the knight.
In vain the steed,—his eyes are blinking,
His chest strains hard, his head is sinking,—
Still hurries, blind, through whirl and rain
In terror, and through night that thickens.
In one last spurt his pace he quickens,
To rest, exhausted, on the plain.

---

[1] The sense of a proverbial couplet, with no English equivalent, which runs literally, 'I come, I come, I won't whistle; but when I catch you I'll not let you go.'

Pushkin

[*Ruslan overcomes the Head and finds the fateful sword underneath it. The Head gives in, and tells his story. He is, it proves, the brother of Chernomor; and the wizard, by a trick, has planted him here; the sword is to be fatal to them. The Head speeds off Ruslan to punish Chernomor. (The story now follows Ratmir, who comes on a magic castle of luxury and is received by maidens.) Ruslan wanders on; and the story returns to the*]

Invisible Lyudmila

And how meanwhile does she, my rare
Lovely princess, Lyudmila, fare?
The magic cap is her salvation,
She fears no wizard's molestation;
She walks unseen; yet, never speaking
And downcast, through the garden flits;
And still she sighs, in spirit seeking
Her own dear friend; and she permits
Forgetfully her dreams to roam
To Kiev and the plains of home.
Father and brothers she embraces;
She sees her youthful playmates' faces
And her old nurses'; all forgot
Her severance, and her captive lot!
But now too swiftly the illusion
Fades, and has left our poor princess
Once more alone and in distress.

All day, in scurry and confusion,
All night, the slaves of that enamoured
Misdoing sorcerer did not dare
Once to sit down, but loudly clamoured

Ruslan and Lyudmila

Through castle, gardens everywhere,
And still the charming prisoner sought.
But all their trouble went for nought;
Lyudmila was amused; and flying,
Would flash to view—without the hat—
Among the groves of faery, crying
'This way, this way, this way, not *that*!'

Then all the mob rushed out to catch her,
But suddenly, again unseen,
With noiseless foot she slipt between
The greedy hands that sought to snatch her;
And every hour, in every place,
They saw a momentary trace;
The gilded fruit upon the bough
That rustled, lo! was disappearing;
Drops from the wellspring tumbled now
Out on the trodden grassy clearing;
'Twas she, as all the castle knew,
Who ate and drank; the thing was true!

And the nights found Lyudmila sleeping,
Hid in a birch or cedar-tree,
One instant, if she might; but she
Was all the time in floods of weeping,
Calling for husband, and for rest,
Tired out, and sorrowing, and yawning;
And rarely, just before the dawning,
With head upon the timber prest,
She dozed, but lightly at the best.
And, when the night-fog just was breaking,
Lyudmila now her way was making
To wash in the chill waterfall.
The dwarf, once looking from his hall

In early morning, saw it spatter
Upward in spray, and fall and scatter,
As troubled by some hand unseen.
But she, as ever sad and yearning,
Roamed up and down those gardens green,
And waited for the night returning.
And often, as the day was closing,
Her sweet voice sounded in their ear;
Often they found a wreath, reposing
Abandoned in a thicket near;
Or else a shred of Persian shawl,
Or tear-stained kerchief, in a ball.

[*Chernomor produces a phantom Ruslan, thus discovering where she is; he traps her in a net and throws her into a magic sleep. He is interrupted by the horn of the true Ruslan.*]

The Air-Fight

Who sounds that trumpet? Who is scaring
The sorcerer now, and summons him
To bloodshed and to battle grim?
Ruslan, with wrath and vengeance flaring!
And near the miscreant's dwelling still
Our warrior waits, below the hill,
His horn its stormy challenge sounding.
The horse grows hot and restive, till
Its mighty hoofs the snow are pounding.
Then, as the prince awaits his foe,
Invisibly a sudden blow
Much like a thunderbolt comes crashing,
Down on the stout steel helmet smashing.
The prince, who dimly upward gazes,

Ruslan and Lyudmila

Sees straight above him high in air
The dwarfish Chernomor, who raises
A hideous mace, and hovers there.
Ruslan, behind his buckler stooping,
Brandished aloft his blade, to hew;
The other in an instant flew
Into a cloud, was lost to view;
Then, with a great noise downward swooping,
He pounced upon the prince anew.
Aside the warrior retreated
Nimbly; the wizard swung—too late,—
The stroke that was to seal his fate,
And fell, and on the snow was seated.
Ruslan said never a word, but straight
Dismounted, hurried to him, clipped him,
And by the long beard fairly gripped him.
The wizard strained and groaned, and lo!
Flew upward, with Ruslan in tow.
The good horse pawed, and watched them go.

The wizard mounts, the clouds enwreathe them;
The hero dangles at his beard;
They fly, with gloomy woods beneath them;
They fly, o'er savage hills upreared;
They fly o'er oceans never sounded,
And doggedly Ruslan still grasps
The villain's beard; his hand around it
Grows numb and rigid as he clasps.
Then, weakened by his voyage airy,
Amazed at that strong Russian arm,
Said the enchanter, sly and wary,
To proud Ruslan: 'No further harm
I do thee now, whate'er befall.
I will forget and pardon all.

Now hear me, prince! I love, in truth,
Thy gallant spirit and thy youth.
I will come down—but on condition——'

    Our prince broke in, would hear no more:
'Be silent, trickster, rogue, magician!
It is not for Ruslan, be sure,
To bargain with a Chernomor,
My wife's tormentor; thou mayst wander
Far as the star of evening yonder,
Yet this dread sword shall punish thee,
And, pirate, thou shalt beardless be!'

    Then Chernomor, his heart constricted
With panic, dumbly vext, afflicted,
Wags his long beard, but still in vain,
A weary dwarf. With might and main
Ruslan holds ever tighter, tweaking
Now and again the wizard's hair.
Thus for two days he doth him bear,
Then sues for mercy, humbly speaking:
'Good knight, take pity, be more tender;
My breath is short, my strength is gone;
Leave me my life, and I surrender;
I will come down to earth upon
Whatever spot thou dost command me.'
—'Ah, now thou tremblest! understand me,
Thou art my slave; be pacified;
Bow to a Russian's might; and land me
Near my Lyudmila, near my bride.'

    [*Ruslan shears off the beard, packs the dwarf in his wallet,
and finds Lyudmila in her trance. Fin appears and tells
him that she shall awake in Kiev. Ruslan takes her and the*

dwarf, and they revisit the Head, who now dies content, on seeing his brother punished. (They come on Ratmir, now happy with a new lady, and friendly.) Meantime Farlaf the boaster, following the guidance of a cat-witch, comes on Ruslan and Lyudmila sleeping. Ruslan has an ominous dream, and Farlaf pierces him, carries off the lady, and makes for Kiev. He there pretends that he has rescued her, and claims her hand. Stir in the city; next morning they see an army of besieging Pechenegs. Fin meantime is in]

The Valley of Death

Where the dry tindery steppes extend
Lonely and mute, and past the end
Of wild hill-chains, where winds and thunders
Keep house and stormily descend,
There lies a secret vale of wonders;
And hither, when the hour is late,
No witches' gaze dare penetrate.
Within that vale two founts are flowing:
One, *Living Water*, gaily going
And gurgling on its pebbled bed;
The other water is the *Dead*.
No cool spring breezes here are blowing;
Here the wind slumbers; all around
Is still; no bird soars up; no sound
Hums in the secular pines; in raging
Hot summer, never a doe, assuaging
Thirst in those hidden streams, is found.
Here, since the world was made, are dwelling
Two silent Spirits, sentinelling;
And here, in peace embosomed deep,
They watch beside those shores of sleep.

[*Fin flies to Ruslan, revives and cures him with the magic water, gives him a magic ring, speeds him to Kiev, and vanishes. Ruslan arrives there the day after the first battle, appears among the Pechenegs* [1] *to rescue the city, and leads the Russians to victory.*]

A Battle

 The day is here; at earliest light
The foe come thronging from the height.
Indomitable squadrons, pouring
In from the plain and seething, all
Flood to the very city wall;
Within, the trumpets loud are roaring.
The ranks in tight array advance,
At the bold adversary dashing;
The fight boils up, the hosts are clashing;
The horses scent the dead, and prance;
The swords upon the armour rattle;
The clouds of arrows hiss and fly;
The low grounds drenched in bloodshed lie;
The horsemen rush to join the battle,
Their squadrons mingle, friend with foe;
And in a serried wall uniting,
Front hews at front, gives blow for blow.
Footman and rider here are fighting,
And there a charger bolts in fear;
Here falls a Pecheneg, and here
A Russian. Thither flee the routed
And yonder is the war-cry shouted.

---

[1] A barbarous nomad race, probably Turkish. About the end of the tenth century they harried Kiev and were repelled by the historical Vladimir, grand duke and saint.

And one drops clubbed to earth, and dies;
A nimble arrow smites another;
One, whom his shield and buckler smother,
Hoofed by a maddened war-horse lies.
Night darkens, ere the fray is done;
And neither they, nor Ours, have won.

[*Later, Ruslan routs the enemy, rides into Kiev, and wakes Lyudmila with the ring. Farlaf is exposed but forgiven; Chernomor, now beardless and harmless, is taken into the palace. Vladimir resumes and finishes the wedding banquet, and*——]

There, in his audience-chamber high,
Feasts with his family, in glory.
— I tell you deeds of days gone by;
From far tradition comes the story.

From POLTAVA

Now in the East another day
Flames, to the din of cannon roaring
On hill and plain; the smoke whirls, soaring
Redly to meet the morning ray.
The ranks are closed; the marksmen scatter
In bushes; see, in ridges set,
The cold steel of the bayonet;
Balls fly, and bullets hiss and patter.
The Swede, long victory's favoured son,
Now rushes trench and blazing gun.
The cavalry are wildly prancing;
The infantry, behind advancing,
In ponderous masses reinforce
The rush and onset of the horse.
O'er all that fateful field of battle
Is dropping fire, and thunderous rattle.
But now the luck of war, behold,
Befriends us, and their Guard retiring
Fall in confusion, and are rolled
In dust and ruin by our firing.
Now Rozen shoulders from the field;
The fiery Schlippenbach must yield;
Troop after troop, we hem the crowded
Lines of the Swede, who see today
The glory of his banners clouded;
And every foot we make of way
By grace of God who guides the fray
Is ours assured.
         And then resounded
With inspiration from on high

Poltava

Descending, Peter's trumpet-cry
'Now, with God's help, to work!'   Surrounded
By followers, the best preferred,
Came Peter, as he spoke the word,
Out of his tent.   His eyes shone brightly,
His face struck terror.   Swiftly, lightly
Moved Peter, wearing, as he trod,
The splendour of the wrath of God.
They bring his trusty horse, a creature
Quiet, yet mettlesome of nature;
It scents the fateful fire, and panting
Quivers in fear, with eyeball slanting;
Then, proud to bear that puissant tsar,
It plunges in the dust of war.

(iii. 153–94.)

From EVGENY ONEGIN

[*The young Evgeny Onegin, dandified, superficially brilliant, sick of the world of fashion and of light loves, disbelieving in love and in general prematurely disenchanted, inherits an uncle's estate in the country and settles upon it, still bored and restless. Another youth, Vladimir Lensky, a poet and enthusiast and idealist, nourished on Goethe and Schiller, joins Onegin the cynic. Lensky is in love with Olga Larin, the younger daughter of a neighbouring family, who keep house in the old Russian style. The elder sister is Tatyana, the heroine of the poem.*]

The Sisters

Charmed while a lad, without a notion
How hearts can suffer, he would gaze
On Olga with a new emotion,
And on her childish sports and ways.
Screened by a guardian oak, he shared them;
Their fathers, friends and neighbours, paired them
And planned the children's wedding-wreath.
There, in her lone retreat, beneath
The humble shelter, overflowing
With charm and innocence for dower,
The parents saw their Olga flower
Just like a hidden lily blowing
Unnoticed, in the thickest grass,
By bees and butterflies that pass.

Our poet found that Olga fired him
With youth's first dream of ravishment.

The thought of Olga still inspired him
And drew his lute's first low lament.
Gone, golden dreams of recreation!
He fell in love with isolation,
And with tranquillity, with night,
With densest woodland, with starlight,
With the moon's lamp in heaven shining;
To whom we oft would dedicate
Our stroll, on misty evenings late,
And wept, to ease our secret pining.
Now, a mere substitute she seems
For our dim, tarnished lantern-gleams.

Always so modest, acquiescent,
And cheerful as the morning skies;
Frank as a poet's life; and pleasant
As lovers' kisses; and with eyes
Of azure like the heavens, and tender;
And smile, and flaxen locks, and slender
Figure, sweet voice, and movements free,
—All this was Olga; you may see,
No doubt, her traits in what romantic
Story you will; I vow to you,
I loved them once myself, 'tis true;
Yet soon they nearly bored me frantic;
Bear, reader, with my taking next
The elder sister for my text.

Her name, Tatyana,[1] be it noted,
Is by our will, and not by chance,
By us for the first time devoted

---

[1] 'Sweet-sounding Greek names, as, for example, Agathon, Thilat, Thedora, Thekla, etc., are only in use with us among the common people' (*Pushkin's note*).

To usage in a mild romance.
Well, 'tis a pleasant name, and ringing,
Although inevitably bringing
The times of old to memory
Or the maids' attic. And yet we
Must own that little taste has brightened
Our choice of names (and as for verse,
I hold my peace, for there 'tis worse).
Skin-deep, no more, are we 'enlightened';
And what is left us of it all
Is merely—to be finical.

Tatyana was her name—so be it;
She had not Olga's pretty face,
So taking, that all men could see it,
Nor her fresh colouring and grace.
She was mute, shy, and melancholy,
Timid as woodland hind; and wholly
A stranger lass she seemed to be
In her own house and family.
And never could her sire, or mother,
Win her caress; she did not care
To join the children's mob, or share
Herself, amid the childish crowd,
Their sports and gambols, like another;
But often by the window lay
And said no word, the livelong day.

And Reverie, her playmate daily
From infancy, brought many a dream
That tinted, to her eyes, more gaily
The village life's too leisured stream.
The needle, her unhardened finger
Knew not; and never would she linger

Bent o'er her frame, with some design
Of silk, to make bare linen fine.
A child betrays our love of ruling;
With her obedient doll will she
Prepare to play propriety
—The great world's law—in jest and fooling;
To dolly, gravely will repeat
The lessons learned at mammy's feet.

But Tanya did not care for nursing,
Young as she was, her doll, or choose
With dolly to be found conversing
On fashions, or the town's last news.
All childish pranks were foreign to her;
Rather would tales of horror woo her
And on her spirit lay their spell
When the dark nights of winter fell.
And when the nurse collected for her
Her little friends, she never ran
To play at 'catch-me-if-you-can'
In the big meadow. It would bore her
To hear the ringing mirth, the noise
Of giddy, romping girls and boys.

She loved the first anticipations,
Seen from the balcony, of day.
The choral dance of constellations
On the horizon pales away,
And the world's rim grows softly clearer
And wafts announce that morn is nearer
And the day slowly comes to birth.
In winter-time, when half the earth

Under the realm of night is shrouded,
Longer and longer sleeps the dawn
In sluggard idleness withdrawn,
In presence of a moon beclouded.
Aroused at the same hour of night,
Tatyana rose by candle-light.

(ii. 21–28.)

[*The friends pay a call on the Larins. Tatyana, who has grown up with her mind full of the romances of the day, sees their ideal hero in Onegin, and loves him passionately at first sight. He is unaware and indifferent.*]

Tatyana and her Nurse

So she, love's quarry, sick and dreary,
Goes in the garden to lament,
And lowers her fixt gaze, too weary
For walking, and too indolent;
When, suddenly, her bosom rises;
A flying flame her cheek surprises;
Breathless, with dazzled eyes, she hears
A noise of thunder in her ears.
Night is at hand; the moon patrolling
Circles the skiey arch remote,
And through the misty trees is rolling
The nightingale's sonorous note.
Tatyana, wakeful, and her nurse
There in the quiet gloom converse.

'Oh, I am sleepless; nurse, sit near me;
Open a window, or I choke!'
—'What ails thee, Tanya?'—'Tired! 'twould cheer me
If of the good old times we spoke.'

—'What should we speak of? I was able
Once to remember many a fable
And deed of long ago; I had
Stories of maids, of spirits bad;
But all things now before me darken;
I have forgotten what I knew.
My turn has come; 'tis bad, but true:
And I am stricken now.'—'But hearken!
Nurse, of thy youth I would be told.
Wert thou in love, in days of old?'

 'Stay, child; folk then were never given
To hearing about love, you see;
—Why, my man's mother, now in heaven,
Would just have been the death of me.'
—'But then thy marriage, nurse, how came it?'
—'Why, God's plain will it was to frame it.
Vanya was younger; I, my dear,
Was only in my fourteenth year.
For two whole weeks the dame was calling [1]
Upon us, to arrange the troth.
At last, my father blessed us both,
And I cried sadly—'twas appalling;
They wept as they undid my hair,
Took me to church, and sang me there.

 'To a strange household I departed;
They took me—but thou dost not hear ...'
—'I am so weary and sore-hearted,
I feel so sick—and nurse, my dear,
I'm fit to sob, I'm near to wailing ...'
—'My child, my child, thou must be ailing.

[1] The professional matchmaker, who goes between the families.

God save thee now and pity thee!
What wilt thou that I do for thee?
I'll sprinkle thee with holy water;
Thou burnest!'—'Not with illness, no!
Nurse dear—I am in love—'tis so!'
—'Now may the Lord be with thee, daughter!'
And with frail fingers, as she prayed,
She signed the cross above the maid.
                              (iii. 16–19.)

Tatyana sends a Letter to Onegin

'That I am writing you this letter
Will tell you all; and you are free
Now to despise me; and how better,
I wonder, could you punish me?
But you, if you are sparing ever
One drop of pity for my fate,
Will not have left me desolate.
I wished at first, believe me, never
To say a word, and then my shame
Had been unknown to you; small blame
Could I have hoped, but once a week
Here in our village, when you came,
To see you, and to hear you speak.
And pass a single word of greeting,
Think of you only, night and day,
And wait—until another meeting.
You are not sociable, they say;
The solitude, the country, bore you.
We are not smart in any way;
But always had a welcome for you.

'Why came you? why to *us*? alone,
In this forgotten hamlet hidden,
I never should have known you, known
This bitterness of pangs unbidden.
And these emotions would have slept,
My soul its quiet ignorance kept:
—So, in due season, might I find,
Who knows? a husband to my mind;
Have been a true wife—to another,
A pious, honourable mother.

' "Another"! . . . I would ne'er have given
To living man, this heart of mine!
This was the will of highest heaven,
This was appointed:—I am thine!
All my past life assurance gave
That we should meet—as though to bind me;
God sent thee here, I know, to find me,
And thou wilt guard me to my grave. . . .

'Thou camest oft in visions to me;
Wert dear, although I knew not thee;
Thy tones reverberated through me,
Thy gaze absorbed, enchanted me
Long since . . . But no, I was not dreaming!
Straight, when thou camest, not in seeming,
I knew thee, I took fire, stood numb,
And my heart told me, "He is come!"
Is it not so? Of old, believing
I heard thee speak, I listened there
To thee in quiet, giving care
To my poor folk, or while relieving
My sick and troubled soul in prayer.

Art thou, today, not he who came,
Flashed through the luminous darkness, nearing
My very pillow? just the same
Beloved vision, reappearing?

'Art thou a guardian angel to me,
Or crafty tempter, to undo me?
Resolve my doubts and my confusion;
It may be, this is all for nought
And an untutored soul's illusion,
And fate quite otherwise has wrought.
But be it thus; henceforth I yield me,
And all my fate, into thy hand;
I weep, and here before thee stand,
Entreating only that thou shield me.

'Conceive it: I am here, and lonely;
None understands me; and if only
My reason were not faint and weak!
But I am lost, unless I speak.
I wait on thee; one look will waken
The hopes with which my heart is shaken;
Or—the dream snap its heavy spell
At one reproach—deserved too well!

'No more of this; I dread to read it;
Yet, though I sink with fear and shame,
Your honour keeps me safe; I plead it,
And to it boldly trust my name.'

Tatyana moaning sits, or sighing,
And grasps the quivering written sheet;

The rosy wafer shrivels, drying
Upon her tongue at fever-heat;
Upon her shoulder she is propping
Her head; the thin light robe is dropping
Down from the charming shoulder.—See,
The radiance of the moon will be
Gone presently, the mists are breaking,
The valley clears; and on the stream
Yonder there steals a silver gleam.
Morning!   The shepherd's horn is waking
The village; now the world's astir.
But Tanya—all is one to her.
      (iii. 31, 32.)

[*Onegin meets her in her garden and in a 'sermon,' priggish but honest, tells her that he cannot accept her love, that he is too world-worn for marriage, and that they would only be unhappy. Tatyana pines; Lensky and Olga are happy, soon to be married. Onegin lives in monotonous comfort.*]

A Winter Scene

Now, this our Northern summer season
Gleams, and is gone—a travesty
Of Southern winters; for some reason
We will not own it—no, not we!
Too soon, with daylight ever sparer
And blinks of sunshine ever rarer,
We feel the tang that autumn brings.
The woods, with mournful murmurings,

Are stript of secrecy and shadow;
And the wild geese, with shrill parade,
Make for the South, in cavalcade;
The low mist settles on the meadow.
A weary time we must await;
November's knocking at the gate!

The dawn comes all in mist, and coldly.
No sound of work—the fields are dumb;
And out upon the highway boldly
The wolf and famished she-wolf come.
The horse that passes knows him, snuffing,
And snorts; the wary traveller, puffing,
Pelts up the hill. At break of day
No herdsman now can drive away
His cattle from the shed; or, calling
At noontide with his horn, can bring
Them round to muster in a ring.
The girl spins in her cottage, drawling
Her song. The matchwood crackles bright,
Good company for wintry night!
(iv. 40–41.)

Another

That year the autumn was belated,
The weather held so long; and still
The world awaited winter, waited
For January to come; until,
On the third night, fell snow. Awaking
Early, Tatyana saw it making
The courtyard and the rooftree white,
And fence and flowerbed; saw the light

Ice-tracery on the panes, the cover
Of silver on the trees; the court
Gay with the magpies and their sport.
The mountains, softly strewn all over,
Sparkled with winter's carpeting.
White, sharp, and clear was everything.

Winter! the peasant's heart now dances;
Again he journeys in his sleigh.
The old mare sniffs the snow, advancing
With shambling trot, as best she may.
The tilted cart is bravely swinging,
The powdery snow from ruts upflinging.
In sheepskin coat and belt of red
The driver perches at its head.
Next, in his little sledge's traces,
Pretending to be horse—and there
Black Puppy sits, for passenger—
With freezing hands, the houseboy races;
The rascal smarts, and grins the more
For mother, threatening at the door.

(v. 1–2.)

Tatyana and Folklore

Tatyana, knowing not the reason
—For she was Russian to the core—
Adored our Russian winter season
In all its beauty, cold and hoar:
The sunny rime, the frosty morning,
The sledges, and the tardy dawning
When the snows gleam with rosy hue;
The misty Christmas evenings, too:

For all the house were solemnising
Those evenings, in the ancient style;
And all the serving-maids, the while,
Of the young ladies were surmising
And yearly promised each one, plain,
A soldier-husband, and campaign.

  Tatyana trusted all traditions
Come down from simple folk of old;
All the cards said, all dreams and visions,
And whatsoe'er the moon foretold.
By tokens she was agitated;
All things she saw prognosticated
Something mysterious; oft her breast
Was by presentiments oppressed.
If puss, upon the stove reposing,
Purred, washed her face with mincing paw,
'Twas a sure sign, Tatyana saw,
Of visitors; and when, disclosing
Her twofold horn, the moon on high
Rode newly in the leftward sky,

  Then Tanya was all pale and shaking;
And did perchance a meteor flee
O'er the dark heavens, and fall, and breaking
Scatter to nought, then hastily
Would Tanya, flustered and excited,
Before that star had yet alighted,
Whisper the wish her heart concealed.
And if a hare, amid the field,
Should streak across her path like lightning,
Or if a monk attired in black
Should meet her on the way,—alack!
Distracted by a sign so frightening,

Full of misgiving and of fear,
She knew calamity was near.

Yet, even while her fears abounded,
A secret pleasure she must own
(For so hath Nature us compounded,
Nature, to contradictions prone).
Yule was at hand,—and such enjoyment!
Guesswork is flighty youth's employment:
Youth has no cause for sorrowing;
For life lies far ahead, a thing
Distant and bright, past all conceiving;
While spectacled old age must peer
And guess, although the grave is near
And all is lost beyond retrieving.
What then? With lispings infantile,
Hope still attends it, to beguile.

And curiously Tanya gazes
Upon the wax that melts and sinks.
The pattern, with its marvellous mazes,
Announces marvels, so she thinks.
The rings come out, in proper order,
From the dish brimming to the border.
She draws a ring; she hums a rhyme,
A ditty of the antique time:
Riches are there for every peasant;
He shovels silver with his spade;
The man we sing to, he is made
In wealth and fame. But sad, unpleasant,
The burden tells of something lost:
The maidens love the *pussy* most.[1]

[1] (*Pushkin's note*): ' "The tom calls his puss to sleep, to the stove niche." A prediction of marriage; the first song presages death.'

A night of frost; no cloud in heaven;
The magic starry choir streams on,
So calm, harmonious, and even . . .
To the wide court is Tanya gone,
Bare-headed, in a kerchief, bending
A mirror on the moon ascending.
Only the mournful moon, alas!
Is quivering in the sombre glass.
—Hist, the snow crackles! Someone coming!
She tiptoes to him, as on wings,
And her low voice more softly rings
Than airs upon a reed-pipe humming.
'*What is your name?*'[1] He looks upon
The maid, and answers, 'Agathon.'

By nurse's counsel, too, the lady
Would tell her fortunes in the night,
And in the bath-house bid make ready
A table laid for two aright,
All quietly. And yet Tatyana
Was scared: and, thinking of Svetlana,[2]
I too was scared:—I know; but see,
Tanya told fortunes—not with me!
The silken girdle soon untying,
Disrobed, she lies upon the bed,
Whilst Lel[3] is hovering overhead.
Her maiden mirror, though, is lying
Beneath the downy pillow deep.
All quiet! Tanya is asleep.

(v. 4–10.)

[1] (*Pushkin's note*) 'This is how they know the name of the future husband.'
[2] Heroine of Zhukovsky's poem, of that name.
[3] See note on *Ruslan*, p. 29.

Tatyana's Dream

    A wondrous dream she now is dreaming:
—That she is walking in a glade
Covered with snow, and swathed, in seeming,
With melancholy mist and shade.
In front, amid the snowdrifts roaring,
A gray and gloomy flood is pouring.
Unfettered now by winter's hand
It whirls and foams along the strand.
Across the torrent laid, united
By icicles, are two thin stakes,
—A bridge of death that thrills and quakes;
And here, bewildered and affrighted,
Tatyana halts, before the hiss
And uproar of that dread abyss.

    And at that plaguy, sundering river
Tatyana can but chafe and chide;
And no one is in sight, to give her
A hand to reach the further side;
When, suddenly, the snowdrift surges!
—Who, who is this that now emerges?
A shaggy, a prodigious bear!
And Tanya screams; he bellows there,
A needle-pointed paw extending
To help her. Gathering all her strength,
She leans upon him; now at length
Her timid footsteps she is bending
Across the stream, with hands that shake.
She's over—Bruin in her wake.

    To look behind, her courage fails her;
With quickened pace she tries in vain

To slip the hairy brute, who trails her
Just like a lackey in her train
And lurches on and growls, past bearing.
Before them is a pinewood, wearing
Its sullen beauty, motionless,
Laden with tufts of snow that press
The boughs to earth. The stars in heaven
Gleam through the birch and aspen crests
And leafless limes; and now there rests
On bush and steep, by tempest driven,
The snow; and it is piled and tost
So deeply, that the track is lost.

 She gains the wood, the bear pursuing,
Up to her knees in crumbling snow;
Now a long, sudden branch is screwing
About her neck, or with a blow
Plucks her gold earrings; now the little
Wet slippers, where the snow is brittle,
Clog her dear feet; now lets she fall
Her kerchief, has no time at all
To lift it. Terrified, and hearing
The pad of Bruin at her heels,
With hands all quivering she feels
Ashamed to lift her skirts. Careering
She flees; he follows, hard upon:
—She flees no more; her strength is gone.

 She drops upon the snow, defenceless,
And nimbly Bruin seizes her,
And she, submissive now and senseless,
Borne onward, cannot breathe or stir.
With her by forest paths he rushes;
Soon a mean hovel through the bushes

Appears, all buried deep and bound
With desert waste of snowdrift round.
One window there is brightly glowing,
And the hut rings with cries and yells.
'Here,' saith the bear, *'my gossip dwells;
Come, warm thee here awhile.'* And going
Straight in the passage, through the door,
He sets her on the threshold-floor.

There she comes to; and falls a-thinking,
And gazes:—vanished is the beast!
Within, are shouts, and glasses clinking,
As though at some huge funeral feast.
No rhyme is here, nor reason! Creeping
And through a crevice softly peeping,
What sees our Tanya now? ah, what?
There, round a table, monsters squat!
One dog-nosed creature horns is wearing;
One has a head like Chanticleer;
There sits a witch, goat-bearded; here
A skeleton, prim and proud of bearing;
A short-tailed dwarf; and here, again,
A thing that is half-cat, half-crane.

But see, more awful, more surprising!
A crayfish on a spider ride;
A skull, above a goose-neck rising
Red-nightcapped, twists from side to side;
And here a windmill dances, clapping
Its sails, and squatting, clattering, flapping.
Barks, whistlings, banging, song, guffaw,
Voices of folk, and hoofs that paw!
But what is Tanya's meditation
When, plain among the guests, is he,

The man she loves, yet fears to see,
The hero of our strange narration,
Onegin! Seated there, askance
Upon the door he casts a glance.

   He drinks—all drink, and howl thereafter;
He makes a sign; all fuss and hum;
He mocks, and all explode in laughter;
He frowns—and all the crowd is mum.
He is the master there, no error!
And Tanya loses half her terror,
And now in curiosity
Opens the door a thought, to see . . .
And lo, a sudden blast comes dashing
And quenches all the candle-lights;
Confusion takes that horde of sprites;
Onegin's eyes with wrath are flashing;
All rise; he rises with a roar
Up from the board, and seeks the door.

   Then panic-stricken, in her hurry
Tatyana struggles to take flight;
But she is powerless; in her flurry
She writhes, and tries to shriek outright;
In vain! Evgeny slams and closes
The door, and that fair maid exposes
Unto the hellish phantoms' gaze.
A wild and violent cry they raise;
And all those eyes, probosces crooked
And tufted tails and tongues that drip
With blood, and each moustachioed lip,
Horns, hoofs, tusks, bony fingers hooked,
All point at Tanya: one and all
Mine! She is mine! No, mine! they bawl.

Evgeny Onegin

No, mine! Evgeny answers grimly;
And, presto! all the gang are flown.
There in the frosty darkness, dimly,
He and the girl abide alone.
And softly then Evgeny sways her [1]
Into a corner, and he lays her
Down on a tottering bench, and stoops;
His head upon her shoulder droops.
Then, while a sudden light is flaring,
Comes Olga; Lensky follows nigh;
Onegin waves an arm on high
And rolls his eyeballs, wildly glaring,
Those guests unbidden to upbraid,
While, all but lifeless, lies the maid.

The jangle swells—Evgeny quickly
Grips a long knife—and straight he fells
Lensky—the awful shadows thickly
Cluster—insufferable yells
Resound—and all the hut is quaking—
And Tanya, horror-struck, is waking . . .
She looks; already it is day
There in her room; a morning ray
Red on the frosted pane is dancing;
And rosier than our northern light
At dawn, and like a swallow's flight,
Comes Olga, through the door advancing.
'Well, well,' she cries, 'and tell me now,
What of thy dream? whom sawest thou?'

(v. 3–21.)

[1] (*Pushkin's note*): 'One of our critics apparently finds in these lines an impropriety, to us unintelligible.'

[*On Tatyana's 'name-day' there is a great festivity at the Larins', and a dance. Onegin, sitting opposite Tatyana, is irritated at the sight of her distress, and in capricious revenge pays too marked attention to the innocent Olga. Lensky, enraged, sends him a challenge by the hand of Zaretsky, an old swashbuckler who has now settled down in the country. On the night before the combat, Lensky makes verses.*]

The Duel

I have his poem; you shall read it;
For, as it chanced, they saved the thing:
—'Ah, whither have ye now receded,
Whither, my golden days of spring?
For me, what is the morrow storing?
How vainly is my gaze exploring!
All, all is wrapt in misty night.
No need; for Fate will judge aright.
Whether I fall, a bullet through me,
Whether it miss,—I still am blest.
The hour to wake, or hour to rest,
Will come—the hour allotted to me.
Blest, if the day to labour calls;
Blest also, if the darkness falls.

'Yes, though the morning ray is sparkling
And day dawns brilliant, yet shall I
Be entering, perhaps, the darkling
Grave, with its shadowy mystery;
And tardy Lethe soon shall cover
The name of the young poet-lover.
The world will not remember me.

—But thou, fair maiden, thou wilt be
By my untimely urn, and by it
Wilt weep, and muse, "His love was great;
To me alone was consecrate
The sad morn of a life unquiet."
—Friend of my heart, for whom I sigh,
Come to me, come! thy spouse am I.'

This penned he, in the *dark, faint* fashion
We style 'romantic'—though I see
No feature of *romantic* passion
Therein—but it concerns not me.
At last, before the dawn was gleaming,
Upon the word *ideal* dreaming
(The word in vogue) he drooped his head
For weariness, and drowsed in bed.
Scarce in oblivion was he falling
Of blissful sleep—his neighbour broke
Into the silent room, and woke
Our Lensky from his slumbers, calling
'Time to be up! by now, be sure,
Onegin waits; 'tis seven, and more.'

But he mistook: Evgeny's sleeping
As sleep the dead; already far
The thinner shades of night are creeping,
And cocks salute the morning star.
The sun wheels high in heaven; yet soundly
Evgeny sleeps, and more profoundly.
A storm of snow is fleeting past
And glitters in the whirling blast.
Still, sleep above Evgeny hovers,
Still he's abed. But in the end
He wakes, the curtained panes uncovers,

And glances—sees that past a doubt
It is high time to sally out.

He rings in haste; and in comes flying
Guillot, his lackey and a Gaul,
Slippers and dressing-gown supplying,
And change of linen brings withal.
Onegin swiftly then attires him,
And bids the man prepare; requires him
To share his drive, and bring away
The case of weapons for the fray.
The sledge stands ready; off he courses,
And in it to the mill they tear.
Behind him must the lackey bear
Lepage's [1] deadly arms; the horses
Are driven to a plot of land
Apart, where two oak saplings stand.

Lensky impatiently had waited
Long, as he leaned upon the weir.
Zaretsky low the millstones rated
(He was a rustic engineer).
Onegin comes, and brings excuses;
'But,' cries Zaretsky, 'where the deuce is
Your second?'—As a duellist
He was a pedant, would insist
On classic forms; of all things dearest
To him was method; he'd allow
Your man to drop—not anyhow,
But on the principles severest
Of art, in old tradition's ways
(Which, in Zaretsky, we must praise).

[1] 'A famous gunsmith' (*Pushkin's note*).

Evgeny Onegin

'*Where,*' says Onegin, 'is my second?
Monsieur Guillot, my friend, is here,
Whom I present.   I had not reckoned
Upon demurs.   He is, I'm clear,
—Though not a man of note, I grant it—
An honest soul.   What more is wanted?'
Zaretsky bit his lip, and heard;
And then Onegin spoke a word
To Lensky: 'Well, and what of starting?'
'Start,' said Vladimir, 'if you will.'
And so they stept behind the mill.
The 'honest soul,' aloof departing,
Talked gravely with Zaretsky; fast
The foes now stand, with gaze down cast.

—Foes! and how long had this estranging
Bloodthirstiness between them flared?
How long since, all their thoughts exchanging,
Their leisure hours as friends they shared,
Their meals, their doings?   Evil-hearted,
As though by hate ancestral parted,
In calm cold blood, they now prepare
To kill each other, as it were
In some insensate, dreadful vision.
And why not part in friendship, ere
Their hands are red—and only care
To laugh the matter to derision?
—But false and foolish shame intrudes
Its terrors, in our worldly feuds.

Behold, the pistols now are gleaming;
The hammer on the ramrod knocks;
Down the cut barrels now are streaming
The bullets; once, have snapt the cocks.

And now the greyish powder scatters
Into the pan, as down it spatters.
The jagged flints, screwed safe below,
Are lifted still.—There stands Guillot
Behind a stump, in consternation.
The fighters cast their cloaks; the due
Paces, in number thirty-two,
Zaretsky, with nice mensuration,
Has taken.   At the further end
With pistols drawn he plants the friends.

   'Approach!'—And regularly, coldly,
Not aiming yet, the combatants
Without a sound, but stepping boldly,
March on; four paces they advance,
Four fatal paces these!   Not waiting,
And never his advance abating,
Evgeny is the first to lift
His pistol quietly.—They shift
Five paces nearer; Lensky closes
An eye, the left—begins to aim
Also; Onegin at the same
Instant has fired.—Thus fate disposes,
And strikes the hour.   The poet lets
His pistol drop—his hand he sets

   Hard to his bosom, never saying
One word, and falls—his clouded eye
No pang, but death itself portraying.
So on a mountain, from on high
A heap of snow we see declining
Slowly, with sunny sparkles shining.
Then, on a sudden stricken cold,
Onegin rushes to behold

The youth—all vainly on him calling.
But he is gone; and he who sung
Has ended all too soon, too young.
One blast—and the fair blossom falling
All withered now, at daybreak, lies;
The flame upon the altar dies!

He lay, he stirred not;—what strange reading,
That peace and languor on his brow!
The wound, that still was steaming, bleeding,
Pierced clean below the breast. Even now,
A moment since, with inspiration
That heart had throbbed, with animation
Of hope, of love, of enmity.
The blood seethed hot, the life beat high.
And now, just like a house deserted,
All dark and still it had become,
Had fallen for ever mute and dumb;
The shutters up, the windows dirtied
With spots of chalk. No host is there,
His traces vanished—God knows where!
(vi. 21–32.)

Evgeny, gripping pistol tightly,
With pangs of sick compunction filled,
On Lensky looks. His neighbour lightly
Pronounces, 'Well? the man is killed.'
'Killed!'—As that hideous word is sounded,
Evgeny shudders, whelmed, confounded;
Goes off, and shouts for aid, while there
The ice-cold body, with due care,
Zaretsky in the sledge is setting.
He drives the ghastly burden home;
The horses scent the dead; white foam

The steely mouthpiece now is wetting;
They rear and struggle, snort and blow,
Then fly, like arrows from the bow.

(vi. 35.)

Lensky's Woodland Grave, visited by Olga and Tatyana

Come, where a brook is swiftly winding
Through half-encircling hills, and past
A lime-tree thicket, and is finding
A river by green fields at last;
Where chants the nightingale, spring's lover,
All night, and where the blossoms cover
The briar, and bubbling waters call.
Here stands a stone funereal
Between two pine-trees antiquated.
The legend tells the passer-by,
'Vladimir Lensky here doth lie';
(The year, his age, are duly dated.)
'Too soon he died, as die the brave;
Have peace, young poet, in thy grave!'

Of old, above that urn so quiet,
An unobtrusive garland hung
Upon the sagging pine-tree by it
And in the morning breezes swung.
Of old, two friends, two women, thither
Would come, at leisure late, together
And in the moonlight vigil keep
And by the tomb embrace, and weep.
Now is that stone, forlorn and lonely,

Forgot; the trodden track is now
O'ergrown; no wreath is on the bough;
And, singing his old ditty, only
The frail, grey-headed shepherd near
Plaits shoes,—his miserable gear.

(vii. 6–7.)

[*Onegin disappears and wanders. Tatyana roams the country in distress, visits his empty house, and at last is taken by her family to Moscow. It is time for her to marry; and she marries a prince, an old friend of Onegin's. Years pass, and Onegin arrives in Moscow to find Tatyana changed into a great lady, the leader of a salon, and coldly polite to him. The tables are turned; he is now in love with her, and, seemingly, is disregarded. At last he writes to her, but receives no reply. One day he comes on her in tears, reading his letter—the old Tatyana once more. But she composes herself, and in a beautiful and dignified speech confesses that she still loves him, though she believes that now he is only in love because she is rich and noted and because he desires a conquest. She cannot forget his former lecture (though he had behaved honourably), and his rejection of her. She will always be true to her husband; and she tells Onegin to go. The poet then dismisses him too, with a farewell to the reader.*]

TALE OF THE TSAR SALTAN, OF HIS SON THE FAMOUS AND PUISSANT CHAMPION GVIDON SALTANOVICH, AND OF THE LOVELY SWAN-PRINCESS

By their window sat and spun
Maidens three; the day was done.
And the eldest maid was saying:
'Were I empress, I'd be laying
Out in state a banquet fine,
For the whole wide world to dine.'
And the second maid was saying:
'Were I empress, I'd be laying
Linen out, and weave by hand,
For the whole world, every strand.'
Then the youngest spoke, the other:
'Were I empress, I'd be mother
Of a hero; I would bear
To our father-tsar an heir.'

Scarce that maid had ended speaking,
When the door went softly creaking,
And the emperor stept inside,
Lord of all that country wide.
All the while they were debating,
He behind the fence was waiting,
And the youngest sister's word
Pleased him best of all he heard.
'Beauteous maiden, happy meeting!
Be my empress!'   Such his greeting.
'Bear me that same hero son
Ere September's out and done.

Tsar Saltan

You, beloved sisters, quitting
This poor chamber, must be flitting
In my train, and follow now—
Follow, too, your sister. Thou
Shalt be cook, and thou, the second,
Lady-webster shalt be reckoned.'

Father-tsar went in the hall;
To the palace hastened all.
Tsar Saltan, not long he tarried;
On that evening he was married.
Noble was the feast; thereat
With his youthful queen he sat.
Then the noble guests attended
To a couch of ivory splendid
Bride and bridegroom, young and fair,
And alone they left them there.
Cook, within the kitchen railing,
Webster at the loom bewailing,
Grudge the good things that befall
Such a spouse imperial.
But the lady, young and royal,
To the word she gave was loyal,
And that night became with child.

These were times of war, and wild.
Tsar Saltan, on point of parting,
On his trusty charger starting,
Bade his queen: 'From every ill
Keep thyself, and love me still.'
While he far away was faring
Long, and pitilessly warring,
Came her time at last; and God
Brought a boy—of two foot odd.

With her babe the empress resting,
Like a mother-eagle nesting,
Sent a rider with a scroll
To rejoice the father's soul.
But, to compass her undoing,
Cook and webster plots were brewing
To forestall that messenger;
Babarikha, dowager,
Grandam, aiding; and another
Was despatched, with this: 'The mother
Yesternight gave birth to one
Neither frog, nor mouse, nor son—
No, nor daughter; but a creature
Monstrous, new, and out of nature.'

When the rider brought that word,
And the tsar, the father, heard,
First he bade him hang, in passion;
Bore himself in strangest fashion,
Yet, for once relenting, gave
These commands unto the slave:
'Wait: the emperor, returning,
Shall adjudge, by law and learning.'

With the writing forth he passed,
Rode, and got him home at last.
Cook and webster and that other,
Babarikha, the queen-mother,
Gave the word to ply him deep,
Got him in a drunken sleep,
Robbed his wallet of the writing,
Planted one of their inditing.
So that day the fuddled man
Brought the order; thus it ran:

Tsar Saltan

'These, to our boyars: Obey ye.
Not an idle hour delay ye.
Queen and brood fling privily
In the bottomless deep sea.'
And the good boyars, they failed not;
Nought would serve; and grief availed not
For their lord and mistress young.
So into her room they flung,
Told how both must meet disaster
At the bidding of the master;
Read the order out; anon
Set the empress and her son
In a barrel; and then thickly
Tarred it over, rolled it quickly,
Drove it duly forth to sea.
'Thus he told us; thus do we.'

In the blue sky stars are flashing;
On the blue sea waves are lashing;
Stormy cloud the sky bedims;
On the sea the barrel swims.
There the queen lies, struggling, straining,
Like a woeful widow plaining.
Every hour the child hath grown
Fast as though a day were flown.
Still she wails; and still he urges,
As the day goes by, the surges:—
'Wave, my wave, beloved of me!
Thou art boisterous and free;
Wheresoe'er thou wilt thou splashest,
Shingle upon shingle dashest,
Flooding all the shores that be,
Hoisting vessels on the sea.

I command thee, do not slay us;
On the dry land wash and lay us!'
There and then the obedient wave
Gently to the foreshore drave
Freight and barrel; left them stranded;
Noiseless ebbed; behold them landed!
Child and queen are safe ashore,
And she feels the earth once more.
—Who from out the cask shall take them?
Surely God will not forsake them?
On his feet the boy stands straight,
At the bottom drives his pate,
Gives a little heave, and asks then,
'How are windows cut in casks, then,
For escape?'—without ado
Bursts the bottom, and comes through.

Now the pair are free to wander.
See, a champaign rises yonder
To a hill with green oaks crowned,
With the blue sea spanning round.
But the son and heir was heedful,
Holding a good supper needful;
Snapped an oaken branch, and so
Bent it in a stubborn bow;
From his cross [1] a silk cord taking,
Strung it on the bow, and breaking
Short a slender reed, made right
A good arrow, sharp and light.
Then he went for quarry forward
To the valley-edges shoreward.

[1] The cross which every Orthodox wears around his neck from a child.

Tsar Saltan

To the beach he scarce had gone,
When he heard—was that a moan?—
Saw the sea disturbed,—and, gazing,
Something evil and amazing:—
In the wave, a swan shows fight,
And above her hangs a kite.
And the poor bird wildly splashes,
And the troubled water lashes;
He his needle-claws outflings,
Whets his gory neb;—then sings
All at once the arrow speeding,
Strikes his crop, and sends him bleeding
Out his life into the flow.
And the prince, with lowered bow,
Sees the creature sink and flutter
With a cry no bird could utter.
And the swan floats round, and still
Pecks that kite of wicked will,
Batters him with wing descending,
Drowns him, for a quicker ending.
Then to the tsarèvich young
Speaks she in the Russian tongue:
'Thou, my prince, wert my salvation,
Mighty for my liberation.
Grieve not that because of me
Thy good shaft lies under sea,
Or that thou must fast to-morrow:
Sorrow proves not always sorrow.
Richly shalt thou be repaid,
And hereafter have my aid.
Saviour of a swan thou seemest,
But a maid to life redeemest;
With thy arrow thou didst smite
An enchanter, and no kite.

Know, that always I shall mind thee;
Be thou where thou mayst, I find thee.
Now, however, homeward get.
Go; sleep sound; no longer fret.'

So flew off the swan enchanted.
Queen and prince held firm, and scanted,
Though a livelong day had passed;
Bedward went, nor broke their fast.
Next the prince, his eyes unclosing,
Shook away his dreams and dozing,
And behold! to his amaze,
A great city met his gaze.
White the walls were, and behind them
Thick the battlements that lined them;
Church and sacred cloister there
Sparkle, turreted in air.
Quick the queen is roused and sighing
Oh! and *ah!* The prince is crying
'Will the thing come true? I see,
Pleasant is my swan with me.'
To the city both betake them,
Cross the barrier; to make them
Welcome, triply surge and swell
Deafening chimes from every bell.
And the folk flood out to meet them;
Holy choirs praise God, and greet them;
In gold chariots to the gate
Comes the court in princely state.
All men praise and honour loudly
That tsarèvich; crown him proudly
With a prince's cap; declare
He is monarch of all there.
License of the queen obtaining,

Tsar Saltan

On that day the prince is reigning
In his capital; thereon
Takes the name of *Prince Gvidon*.

   Breezes on the water shifting
Landward urge a vessel drifting,
Bellying out her canvas brave
As she skims along the wave.
On the deck the shipmen teeming
Wonder if awake or dreaming
Such a marvel they behold
On that island, known of old:—
Strongly gated quays, and gilded
Towers; a city newly builded!
Cannon flaming from the quay
Bid the ship put in from sea;
And the strangers by the gateway
Moor; the prince invites them straightway,
Gives them food and drink, and then
Thus makes question of the men:
'Merchants, what are ye exchanging?
Whither may ye now be ranging?'
Then the sailor-men speak out:
'We have sailed the world about:
Now in sables we have traded,
Now in foxes dusky-shaded.
Past the island of Buyan,
To the realm of famed Saltan
Now due eastward we are wending.
Time is up; our trip is ending.'
'Happy journey, every man,
To the famous tsar Saltan
Over sea and ocean faring!'
So the prince gave word, declaring:

'Do him reverence from me!'
Then they went, and, gazing, he
Watched them far, beheld them vanish,
Sad with thoughts he might not banish.
Look! the snowy swan, aswim
On the billows, calls to him
'Hail, my lovely prince, good morrow!
Tell me, tell me, prince, thy sorrow?
Why art thou so silent, say,
Downcast as a rainy day?'
'I've a weary grief devouring,
All my manhood overpowering.
Would I might my father see!'
Dolefully thus answered he.
But the swan said, 'Art thou minded
To pursue the ship? behind it
Flit, and be a midget, since
This is all thy woe, my prince!'
Then she waved her wings, and scattered
Noisily the wave, and spattered
Him with spray from top to toe.
In a single instant, lo,
To a dot he shrank and minished,
Was a midge; the change was finished.
Piping soft, away flew he,
Caught the vessel on the sea,
Lighted gently, to discover
A good cranny, and took cover.

Past the island of Buyan,
To the realm of famed Saltan
Gaily onward flies the trader,
Gaily hums the breeze to aid her;
See, already looming nigher

Is the land of her desire!
Soon the strangers, newly landed,
To the palace are commanded,
And behind them to the king
Our adventurer takes wing.
There he sees, in gold all shining,
But with countenance repining,
Crowned and throned above them all,
King Saltan within his hall.
Cook and webster and that other,
Babarikha the queen-mother,
Pin their looks upon the king,
Squatting round him in a ring.
Then he calls the guests and seats them
At his board; with question greets them:
'Master-merchants, where go ye?
Sailed ye long? and over sea
Fared ye well? Or lived ye poorly?
In the world are wonders, surely?'
Then the sailor-men speak out:
'We have sailed the world about.
Overseas we lived not poorly;
Here was a world's wonder, surely?—
Once an island in the deep
Lay unpeopled, barren, steep,
Blank and level; on it growing
Was a single oak-tree showing.
There to-day a city new
With a palace stands to view.
Golden-steepled churches cap it,
Towers ascend, and gardens lap it.
There sits prince Gvidon, and thence
Sends to thee his reverence.'
At the tale astonished duly,

'If I live,' the tsar said, 'truly
I will see that wondrous isle,
Have Gvidon my host awhile.'
Cook and webster and the other,
Babarikha, the queen-mother,
All were loth to let him so
To that isle of wonders go.
Said the cook, malignly winking
To her fellows, 'We are thinking
That a city by the sea
Surely is a prodigy!
Hear, now, of no paltry wonder:—
In a wood a pine, whereunder
Sings a squirrel rhyme on rhyme,
Nibbling filberts all the time:
Common filberts they are not, sir;
Each a golden shell has got, sir;
Kernels, of pure emerald:
Which a wonder may be called.'
Tsar Saltan sat there, astounded;
But the midge, in wrath unbounded,
At his auntie drove his sting,
In her right eye plunged the thing.
And the cook went pale, and wried her
Visage, swooning; and beside her
Slave and sister, mother too,
With a shriek the midge pursue.
'Insect double-damned!' they fidget,
'We will show thee . . . !' but the midget
Calmly through the casement flees
To his home beyond the seas.

Prince again, the shore he paces;
Still the azure sea he faces.

Tsar Saltan

Look! the snowy swan, aswim
On the billows, calls to him:
'Hail, my lovely prince, good morrow!
Tell me, tell me, prince, thy sorrow?
Why art thou so silent, say,
Downcast as a rainy day?'
Then he answers, 'Ay, a dreary
Grief consumes me; I am weary
To discover, if I could,
One great marvel:—in a wood
Somewhere stands a pine, whereunder
(Hark you, 'tis no paltry wonder)
Chants a squirrel rhyme on rhyme,
Nibbling filberts all the time:
Common filberts they are, not, ma'am;
Each a golden shell has got, ma'am;
Kernels of pure emerald, too!
—Ah, the tale may not be true!'
But the swan replies, 'No fable
Is that squirrel; I am able
Of this marvel to make sure.
Prince, dear heart, lament no more;
Hold; for I with joy will lend thee
Any service, to befriend thee.'

So with heart uplifted high
Home he goes, and drawing nigh
The wide courtyard, lo! is gazing
On a fir of height amazing
Where a squirrel, before all,
Gnaws the golden nuts that fall,
Out of each an emerald shelling,
And the empty husks is telling

Into many an even pile,
Chanting, whistling all the while
To those noble folk a ditty:
*Is it in the garden pretty,
Or the kitchen-plot?* Gvidon,
Wondering sorely, thanks the swan:
'Lord, bestow on her such blessing
Even as I am now possessing!'
For the squirrel then he bade
That a crystal house be made;
Set a clerk to make an entry
Strict, of every nut; a sentry
Also at the doorway pitched.
—Squirrel honoured, prince enriched!

   Breezes on the water shifting
Landward urge a vessel drifting,
Raising up her canvas brave
As she skims along the wave
Past the island cliff-defended,
Past the city large and splendid.
Cannon flaming from the quay
Bid the ship put in from sea.
Then the merchants by the gateway
Moor; the prince invites them straightway,
Gives them food and drink, and then
Thus makes question of the men:
'Merchants, what are ye exchanging?
Whither may ye now be ranging?'
And the sailor-men speak out:
'We have sailed the world about;
All the while in horses trading,
Stallions from the Don our lading.
Past the island of Buyan

To the realm of famed Saltan
Far the path that we are wending.
Time is up; our trip is ending.'
'Happy journey, every man,
To the famous tsar Saltan
Over sea and ocean faring!'
So the prince gave word, declaring
'Homage take from Prince Gvidon
To the tsar upon his throne.'

Then the merchants bowed, departed,
Straight upon their voyage started.
Seaward stept the prince; thereon
Through the waters rode the swan.
'Ah,' he prayed, 'my soul is longing,
Swept away by wishes thronging . . .'
In a moment, as before,
She besprinkled him all o'er,
And the prince became a fly then,
And between the sea and sky then
Winged away, and on the ship
Lighted, in a chink to slip.

Past the island of Buyan
To the realm of famed Saltan
Gaily onward flies the trader,
Gaily hums the breeze to aid her.
See, already looming nigher
Is the land of her desire!
Soon the merchants, newly landed,
To the palace are commanded,
And behind them to the king
Our adventurer takes wing.

There he sees, in gold all shining,
But with countenance repining,
Crowned and throned above them all
Tsar Saltan within his hall.
Webster; wry-faced cook; that other,
Babarikha the queen-mother,—
Glower like toads upon the king,
Squatting round him in a ring.
Then he calls the merchants, seats them
At his board, with question greets them:
'Strangers, masters, where go ye?
Sailed ye long? and on the sea
Fared ye well?   Or lived ye poorly?
In the world are wonders, surely?'
Then the sailor-men speak out:
'We have sailed the world about;
Overseas we lived not poorly;
Here was a world's wonder, surely:—
On the deep an island lies;
There we saw a city rise;
Golden-steepled churches cap it,
Towers ascend, and gardens lap it.
By a palace is a fir
And a house of crystal, sir;
There a squirrel tame is thriving
And what tricks is she contriving!
She is chanting rhyme on rhyme,
Nibbling filberts all the time—
Common filberts they are not, sir!
Each a golden shell has got, sir!
Kernels, too, of emerald pure.
Guarded there, she sits secure;
Henchmen sundry service tender,
And a clerk is set to render

Count of every nut; at hand
Doing honour, soldiers stand,
Cast those shells in coin, and send them
Round, for all the world to spend them.
Maidens too the emeralds strow
Into padlockt stores below.
All are rich men in that islet,
Nobly housed; no huts defile it.
There sits Prince Gvidon, and thence
Sends to thee his reverence.'
At the tale astonished duly,
'If I live,' the tsar said, 'truly
I will see that wondrous isle,
Have Gvidon my host awhile.'
Cook and webster and that other,
Babarikha the queen-mother,
All are loth to let him so
To that isle of wonders go.
And the webster with a lurking
Snigger to the tsar said, smirking:
'Was it wondrous, what they saw?
Did a squirrel pebbles gnaw,
Gold about at random shaking,
Emeralds in bunches raking?
Be it lies or be it truth,
We are not amazed, in sooth.
For the world a greater wonder
Holds:—a sea that swells in thunder,
Boils tempestuously o'er,
Floods on a deserted shore,
Sunders, noisily careering.
See, upon that shore appearing,
Blazing fierily, there be
Scale-clad champions, thirty-three!

Each is comely, each defiant,
Each a pickt and youthful giant;
All of even height; one more
Follows—uncle Chernomor.
Say now, is not this thing rarely
Wonderful, to call it fairly?'
And the guests, who have the wit
Not to cross her, silent sit.
Tsar Saltan is sore astounded;
But Gvidon, in wrath unbounded,
In a flash, a buzzing fly,
Lights on auntie's leftward eye;
And that webster paled, to find it
Instantly and wholly blinded.
'Catch him, catch him,' still they yell;
'Squash him, squash him, squash him well!
Now we have him; stay, keep still there!'
—Calmly, past the window-sill there,
To his heritage now flees
Prince Gvidon, beyond the seas.

By the shore the prince is pacing,
Ever on the blue sea facing;
Look! the snowy swan, aswim
On the billows, calls to him:
'Hail, my lovely prince, good morrow!
Tell me, tell me, whence thy sorrow?
Why art thou so silent, say,
Downcast as a rainy day?'
Then he answers, 'Ay, a dreary
Grief consumes me; I am weary
For a marvel; would there were
Such a windfall, for my share!'
'Tell me, what might be that wonder?'

'—Somewhere, ocean swells in thunder,
Boils tempestuously o'er,
Floods on a deserted shore,
Spills, in noisy spray careering.
And upon that shore appearing,
Blazing fierily, there be
Scale-clad champions, thirty-three.
Each is comely, each defiant,
Each a pickt and youthful giant,
All of even height; one more
Follows—uncle Chernomor.'
'Here is nothing to disquiet;
Dear one, be not troubled by it,'
So the swan replies; 'for well
Know I that same miracle.
Why, those knights, whom ocean mothers,
Are my true-begotten brothers.
Grieve not; go; the brethren wait;
Give them welcome at thy gate.'

Then he sat, no longer troubled,
In his tower; the waters bubbled;
On the sea his eyes he turned;
Suddenly the ocean churned,
Loudly splashed, and fled, and parted.
On the foreshore up there started
Each one blazing fierily,
Scale-clad champions thirty-three.
Two and two they march; conveying
Citywards the troop, with graying
Locks that glitter, Chernomor,
That good uncle, goes before.
From his tower the prince came posting,
Those dear visitors accosting.

Pushkin

Swiftly scurried up the folk;
To the prince the uncle spoke:
'Bidden by the swan, we landed;
Straitly she hath us commanded
That we guard thy glorious town
And patrol it, up and down.
We are daily now to sally
From the ocean wave, and rally,
Never failing, one and all,
By thy lofty city wall.
Soon we meet again; now leave us;
We must forth to sea, for grievous
Unto us is earthly air.'
One and all, they homeward fare.

   Breezes on the water shifting
Landward urge a vessel drifting,
Raising up her canvas brave
As she skims along the wave
Past the island cliff-defended,
Past the city large and splendid.
Cannon flaming from the quay
Bid the ship put in from sea.
Then the merchants by the gateway
Moor; the prince invites them straightway;
Gives them food and drink, and then
Thus makes question of the men:
'Merchants, what are ye exchanging?
Whither may ye now be ranging?'
And the sailor-men speak out:
'We have sailed the world about;
Virgin silver, gold, and bladed
Steel are wares that we have traded.

Tsar Saltan

Past the island of Buyan
To the realm of famed Saltan
Far the path that we are wending.
Time is up; our trip is ending.'
'Happy journey, every man,
To the famous tsar Saltan
Over sea and ocean faring!'
So the prince gave word, declaring
'Homage take from prince Gvidon
To the tsar upon his throne.'

   Then the merchants bowed, departed,
Straight upon their voyage started.
Seaward stept the prince; thereon
Through the waters rode the swan.
'Ah,' he cried, 'My soul is longing,
Swept away by wishes thronging . . .'
In a moment, as before,
She besprinkled him all o'er;
There and then he shrank and minished
To a humble-bee; 'twas finished;
Flying, droning, off went he,
Caught the vessel on the sea,
Lighted softly, to discover
Aft a cranny, and took cover.

   Past the island of Buyan,
To the realm of famed Saltan
Gaily onward runs the trader,
Gaily hums the breeze to aid her.
See, already looming nigher
Is the land of her desire!
Soon the merchants newly landed
To the palace are commanded,

And behind them to the king
Our adventurer takes wing.
There he sees, in gold all shining,
But with countenance repining,
Crowned and throned above them all
Tsar Saltan within his hall.
Cook, and webster, and that other,
Babarikha, the queen-mother,
All the trio, in a ring,
Gaze, foursquare, upon the king.
Then he calls the merchants, seats them
At his board, with question greets them:
'Merchants, masters, where go ye?
Sailed ye long, and on the sea
Fared ye well? or lived ye poorly?
In the world are wonders, surely?'
Then the sailor-men speak out:
'We have sailed the world about;
Overseas we lived not poorly;
Here was a world's wonder, surely:—
On the deep an island lies;
There a city doth arise;
And each day there comes a wonder:
For the ocean swells in thunder,
Boils tempestuously o'er,
Floods on a deserted shore,
Spills, in noisy spray careering.
Then upon that shore appearing,
Blazing fierily, there be
Scale-clad champions thirty-three.
Each is comely, each defiant,
Each a pickt and youthful giant;
All of even height; one more,
Ancient uncle Chernomor,

With them from the ocean sallies,
And in twos the troop he rallies
To protect that island-town
And patrol it up and down.
Never was a guard securer,
Braver, busier, or surer.
There sits Prince Gvidon, and thence
Sends to thee his reverence.'

   At the tale astonished duly,
'If I live,' the tsar said, 'truly
To that wondrous isle I'll come,
Guest of Prince Gvidon.'   But mum
Cook and webster sit; that other,
Babarikha the queen-mother,
Snickering cries, 'Shall sailor-men
With this tale amaze us, then?
People out of ocean strolling
Wander prowling and patrolling!
Whether lies or truth they tell,
Here I see no miracle.
Can such marvels be? a new one
I will tell ye, and a true one:—
Over sea a princess stays;
None from her can take his gaze;
She bedims the sun in heaven;
She illumes the earth at even;
Moonbeams in her tresses are;
On her forehead burns a star;
And herself, she sails before ye
Like a peafowl in her glory;
When she speaks, her accents seem
Like the warble of a stream.
Say now, is not this thing rarely

Wonderful, to call it fairly?'
And the guests, who have the wit
Not to cross her, silent sit.
Tsar Saltan is sore astounded;
But the prince, his wrath unbounded
Reining, at his grandam flies,
But he spares her ancient eyes.
Round he twirls, and drones, and flounces,
Straight upon her nose he pounces,
And that nose the hero stings;
Up a mighty blister springs.
Then once more alarm is sounded:
'Help—in Heaven's name—confound it!—
Catch him, catch him!' now they yell,
'Squash him, squash him, squash him well!
Now we have him—stay, be still there!'
But the humble clears the sill there;
To his heritage he flees,
Calmly flitting overseas.

 By the shore the prince is pacing,
Ever on the blue sea facing.
Look! the snowy swan, aswim
On the billows, calls to him:
'Hail, my lovely prince, good morrow!
Tell me, tell me, whence thy sorrow?
Why art thou so silent, say,
Downcast as a rainy day?'
'I am wretched, and a dreary
Grief consumes me; I am weary
Watching other people wed,
All but me——', he sadly said.
'But who is she? by what token
Shalt thou know her?' 'Men have spoken

Of a princess. Where she dwells,
The beholder sees nought else.
She bedims the sun in heaven;
She illumes the earth at even;
Moonbeams in her tresses are;
On her forehead burns a star;
And herself, she walks before ye
Like a peafowl in her glory;
When she speaks, her accents seem
Like the warble of a stream.
Only—is this truth or error?'
He awaits her word, in terror.
Silently the snowy swan
Mused awhile, but spoke anon:
'Such a maid there is; but take her
Once to wife, thou canst not shake her
Like a mitten from thy wrist;
No, nor like a girdle twist.
Hear my counsel; thou shalt profit,
So thou wilt avail thee of it:
Ponder all things; hesitate,
Lest repentance come, too late.'
But he swore he would not tarry;
Time was ripe for him to marry;
He had turned it every way
In his thoughts; was ready, nay,
Passionately yearned to wander
After that fair princess yonder;
Fain to trudge it, if need be,
To the world's extremity.
Then the swan—profoundly sighed she—
'Why so far afield,' replied she,
'For thy princess? I am she;
Here behold thy destiny.'

Then, her pinions upward flinging,
Over the wide water swinging,
Down she stooped upon the strand,
Hid her in a bush at hand,
Gave a shake and gave a shiver,
Turned a princess, with one quiver.
Moonbeams in her tresses are;
On her forehead burns a star;
And the lady, in her glory
Like a peafowl walks before ye;
When she speaks, her accents seem
Like the warble of a stream.
Then and there the prince enfolds her
To his bosom white, and holds her;
Then to his dear mother he
Leads her quickly; on his knee
Falls, and thus begins entreating:
'Sovereign lady-mother, greeting!
This my chosen bride shall be
Duteous daughter unto thee.
Grant this boon, that we, possessing
Thy good leave and marriage-blessing,
May in peace and concord live;
So, thy benediction give.'
Then an ikon she extended
Wonder-working, o'er their bended
Heads, and wept, and spoke: 'The Lord
You, my children, shall reward.'
But the prince, not long he tarried,
To the princess he was married,
And they entered on their life,
Waiting increase, man and wife.

Tsar Saltan

Breezes on the water shifting
Landward urge a vessel drifting,
Bellying out her canvas brave
As she skims along the wave
Past the island cliff-defended,
Past the city large and splendid.
Cannon flaming from the quay
Bid the ship put in from sea;
And the merchants by the gateway
Moor; the prince invites them straightway,
Gives them food and drink, and then
Thus makes question of the men:
'Merchants, what are ye exchanging?
Whither may ye now be ranging?'
And the sailor-men speak out:
'We have sailed the world about;
Contraband has been our lading.
Past the island of Buyan
To the realm of famed Saltan
On a far road we are wending,
Eastward, home; our trip is ending.'
'Happy journey, every man,
To the famous tsar Saltan
Over sea and ocean faring!'
So the prince gave word, declaring,
'Mark, your sovereign made a vow
He would be my guest; till now
Never has he stirred; remind him
Of that promise, when ye find him.
Take him homage, too, from me.'
So they went their ways; but he
This time stayed at home, nor started;
Would not from his wife be parted.

Past the island of Buyan,
To the realm of famed Saltan
Gaily onward runs the trader,
Gaily hums the breeze to aid her.
Now the old familiar shore
Looms in sight for them once more,
And the strangers, newly landed,
To the palace are commanded,
And the emperor they behold
Sitting there and crowned with gold.
Cook, and webster, and that other,
Babarikha the queen-mother,
All the trio, in a ring,
Gaze, foursquare, upon the king.
Then he calls the merchants, seats them
At his board, with questions greets them:
'Merchants, masters, where go ye?
Sailed ye long? and on the sea
Fared ye well? or lived ye poorly?
In the world are wonders, surely?'
Then the sailor-men speak out:
'We have sailed the world about;
Overseas we lived not poorly;
Here was a world's wonder, surely:—
On the deep an island lies;
There a city doth arise;
Golden-steepled churches cap it;
Towers ascend, and gardens lap it.
By the palace is a pine,
And a mansion crystalline;
There a squirrel tame is thriving
And such tricks is she contriving!
She is chanting rhyme on rhyme,
Nibbling filberts all the time;

Common filberts they are not, sir;
Kernels too, of emerald pure;
Each a golden shell has got, sir!
Her they pet, and keep secure.

And there is a further wonder:
There the ocean swells in thunder,
Boils tempestuously o'er,
Floods on the deserted shore,
Spills, in noisy spray careering;
And upon that shore appearing,
Blazing fierily, there be
Scale-clad champions, thirty-three.
Each is comely, each defiant,
Each a pickt and youthful giant,
All of even height; one more
Follows, uncle Chernomor.
Never was a guard securer,
Braver, busier, or surer.
With the prince a bride there stays;
None from her can take his gaze;
She bedims the sun in heaven;
She illumes the earth at even;
Moonbeams in her tresses are;
On her forehead burns a star.
Prince Gvidon that city proudly
Rules, and all men praise him loudly.
And he sends thee homage now,
Yet he blames thee: "Where's thy vow
Soon to be our guest, nor linger;
Yet thou never stirrest finger!" '

Then the tsar could not forbear
Longer; bade the fleet prepare.

Cook, and webster, and that other,
Babarikha the queen-mother,
All were loth to let him so
To that isle of wonders go.
But the monarch, nothing heeding,
Silenced then and there their pleading,
Saying, 'Is Saltan a child
Or a tsar?', and never smiled;
Stampt, and cried, 'I sail this morning!'
Left them; slammed the door, in warning.

    Prince Gvidon, all silently
At his window watched the sea;
Not a murmur, or a lashing
Wave, but just a gentle plashing!
But upon the distance blue
Ships were swimming into view:
'Twas the emperor's fleet in motion
Coming o'er the level ocean.
Then the prince Gvidon upsprang,
Thunderous his summons rang:
'Mother of my heart, come hither!
Thou too, young princess; and thither
Turn your eyes, upon the sea;
'Tis my father comes to me.'
And he sees the fleet draw nearer;
Points a spyglass, marks it clearer;
Sees on deck the emperor pass
Spying at them through his glass.
Cook and webster and the other,
Babarikha the queen-mother
By his side bewildered stand
At that unfamiliar land.
Guns flame out from every barrel,

Tsar Saltan

Every belfry chimes a carol.
Prince Gvidon goes down, and he
Meets the tsar beside the sea,
Cook and webster and that other,
Babarikha the queen-mother.
Quickly he the tsar has brought
To the city, saying nought.

To the palace all go straightway.
Armour gleams beside the gateway.
There the emperor can see
Thirty champions and three.
Each is comely, each defiant,
Each a pickt and youthful giant;
All one stature; and one more
Follows, uncle Chernomor.
Next, the tsar the court is treading,
Where, beneath a pine high-spreading
Chants a squirrel rhyme on rhyme,
Nibbling gold nuts all the time,
Out of each an emerald cropping,
In a sack the jewel dropping;
And the spacious court is strewn
With the golden husks alone.
Further still—on what amazing
Princess are the strangers gazing?
Moonbeams in her tresses are;
On her forehead burns a star,
And herself she walks before ye
Like a peafowl in her glory,
And her prince's mother leads.
And the tsar, he gazes, heeds,
Knows them both; his heart is leaping;
'What is here?' he cried, and weeping

Melted, and his breath he drew
Hard and heavily, and knew
Her, his queen, and quickly caught her
To him, and his gallant daughter
And his son. To board they fared
And a noble banquet shared.
Cook and webster and that other,
Babarikha the queen-mother,
Into corners scampered round;
Hardly might those three be found.
Then they broke in sobs and moaning,
All their past transgressions owning,
And the tsar, so glad was he,
Merely banished home the three.
And they bore to bed, half-drunken,
Tsar Saltan, when day was sunken.

I drank beer, drank mead; and yet
Hardly were my whiskers wet.

TALE OF THE DEAD PRINCESS AND THE SEVEN CHAMPIONS

 Once there was a king, who started
Journeying; from his queen he parted;
And she watched, a lonely thing,
At her window for her king.
Morn and eve she watched and waited;
Still the plain she contemplated
Till her eyes were sore, from white
Daybreak to the fall of night.
Never a sign of him, her lover!
All the earth is whitened over,
And the spinning snowstorms fall
On the plains; and that is all.
And her eyes she never raises
From the plains; nine months, she gazes.
—God, ere Christmas eve is morn,
Brings a gift: a girl is born.

 In the morning early, homing
From afar where he was roaming,
Long awaited with desire,
Came at last the king and sire.
Just a look was his to capture;
But she could not bear the rapture;
Deeply, heavily she sighed;
Near the hour of mass, she died.

 Inconsolably, in seeming,
Flew a year of barren dreaming.

Kings are frail, like other men;
Wedded was the king again.
Youthful was the queen he newly
Took to wife; I tell you truly,
She was shapely, white, and tall;
She was first, in wit and all;
Yet a captious, wilful spirit,
Proud, and envious of merit.
She for dowry of her own
Brought a looking-glass alone:
One of strange, peculiar fashion,
With the gift of conversation.
She was never kind or gay
When that mirror was away;
With it, pleasantly she jested;
Preened herself, and thus addressed it:
'Mirror, mirror, let me hear
Nothing but the truth, my dear!
Tell me, am I sweetest, fairest?
Are my red and white the rarest?'
And the mirror still replies,
'Nay, be sure that none denies
Thou art sweetest, thou art fairest,
And the rosiest and the rarest.'
Then the queen in laughter breaks,
And her shoulders shrugs and shakes,
Snaps rejoicingly her fingers,
Winks, and blinks, and proudly lingers
Gazing, with a sidelong pace,
In the mirror at her face.

Silently, with none beholding,
Was the young princess unfolding
All the while; and grew, each hour,

The Dead Princess

Till at last the bud was flower.
Black her brows, and pale her features;
She was gentlest of all creatures.
Seeking her a husband, they
Found a prince, young Elisey.
Message came; the king consented,
And for portion he presented
Seven market-towns; nay more,
Roomy chambers, seven score.

   Now the queen has got upon her
All her finery, in honour
Of the marriage-eve; and now
She bespeaks the mirror: 'Thou,
Tell me, am I sweetest, fairest?
Are my red and white the rarest?'
But the mirror now replies:
'Thou art lovely, none denies;
But the sweetest, rosiest, fairest
Is the princess, and the rarest.'

   How the queen recoils and springs,
Brandishes her arms, and flings
Down the mirror, on it tramping
With her booted heel, and stamping!
'Nasty, spiteful glass, I see
Thou art telling lies to me!
Would she rival me! I'll wholly
Soon dispose of such a folly!
What a creature she is grown!
Why, her mother, it is known,
When with child, on snow was gazing;
So—she's white! Is that amazing?

Nay, but tell me: how should she
Overpass, in sweetness, me?
Journey all our kingdom over,
Though the whole wide world thou cover,
I'm the peerless one confest;
I of all am loveliest.
Tell me!' Still the glass said, 'Fairer,
Rosier is the bride, and rarer.'

  So, no help! the lady next,
With the blackest envy vext,
Flings the glass beneath the benches,
Calls, amongst her chamber-wenches,
One Chernavka; bids her bear
Into some deep woody lair
That princess, and tightly bind her
Where the hungry wolves may find her
Underneath a pine alive
And devour her.

          Now, to strive
With an angry dame is idle.
Not the Devil her can bridle.
Through the wood Chernavka passed
With the maid so far at last,
That the maid, the truth descrying,
Was for terror all but dying,
And besought her: 'Precious one,
Say, what evil have I done?
Do not be my death; and, mind me,
Good and gracious shalt thou find me
On the day that I am queen.'

The Dead Princess

But Chernavka love unseen
Bore her, neither bound nor slew her;
Left her free, made answer to her,
'God be with thee; never grieve';
Homeward then she took her leave.
'So, now tell me where the maid is,
That most beauteous of ladies,'
Asks the queen; the wench replies,
'In the wood alone she lies;
Beasts will catch and claw her, surely,
By the elbows lasht securely.
She will die the easier; less
Are her sufferings and distress.'

Now the rumours ring and thicken
Of the lost princess; and stricken,
Pining for her, sits the king.
Elisey, petitioning
God with heart and soul, goes questing
On the highway, never resting
Till he find his promised wife
Young and fair, his very life.

But that young and lovely lady
Strayed about the forest shady,
Until daybreak threading it.
On a mansion then she lit,
Where a dog ran forward baying.
Then it ceased, and fell to playing;
Through the gate her way she found;
In the court was not a sound;
And the dog behind her wheeling
Fawned; and then the princess, stealing

Pushkin

Gently, mounted up the stair,
Grasped the door-ring hanging there,
And the door swung open lightly;
In a room illumined brightly
Next the princess found herself.
On the stove were tiles of delf
Made to lie on; pictures holy,
Oaken table, benches lowly
Laid with rugs, were there; and kind
Living people she would find,
Surely?—none to harm a woman.
Yet she noted nothing human.
Round the house the princess paced,
All things in good order placed,
To the Lord a taper kindled,
Lit the stove whose warmth had dwindled,
To an attic upward sped,
Laid her softly down to bed.

Now the time to eat is coming;
Footsteps in the court are drumming.
Seven champions enter then,
Ruddy, bushy-whiskered men.
'All is wondrous bright and clean here,'
Says the eldest; 'who hath been here?
Who hath set the room so straight?
Someone doth the hosts await.
—Ay, but who? come forth and greet us!
Friendlike, honourably meet us!
Art thou aged? we will call
Thee our uncle, once for all.
If some ruddy lad or other,
Thou shalt have the name of brother.

The Dead Princess

If an ancient dame, then we
Will as mother honour thee.
If a comely maid thou prove thee,
Be our sister; we will love thee.'

And the princess issued thence,
Did her hosts due reverence,
Made a low, deep inclination,
Blushed, and faltered explanation
How beneath their roof she got
As a guest, though bidden not.
As the champions listened to her,
For a princess straight they knew her.
In a nook they set her there,
Served her with a pasty fair,
Poured a brimming cup, to stand
On a salver at her hand.
But the lady, with a sign,
Waved away the emerald wine;
Broke a corner of the pasty,
Nibbled at a morsel hasty;
But was wayworn, made request
For a bed, to take her rest.
Then the maiden they invited
To an upper room, well lighted,
And they left her there alone.
To her slumbers she is gone.

Like a flash the days go sliding;
Still the young princess is biding
In the wood; not wearisome
Is the seven champions' home.
Ere the dawn, in friendly rally
Out the brethren riding sally;

Take an airing, to let fly
At the grey-winged duck; or try,
All for sport, their sinews, dropping
Mounted Saracens, or lopping
Some broad-shouldered Tartar's pate;
Or from woods they extirpate
Pyatigorsk Circassians straying.
And the lady, still delaying,
Tarries in the room alone,
Keeping house while they are gone;
Makes all trim, prepares the dishes.
Never do they cross her wishes,
Never does she them gainsay.
Day in this wise follows day.

    Now their hearts they all had given
Unto that dear maid.   The seven
Brothers came one morn to her
Ere the sun was well astir.
Said the eldest: 'We have told thee
How we all a sister hold thee,
All the seven; yet we all
Love thee; each one fain would call
Thee his wife, but that we may not.
So, for love of heaven, delay not;
Somehow set our hearts at rest;
Be the wife of one—the best,
To the six a sister loving.
—Why that headshake unapproving?
Wilt not have us?   Is the ware
Not for purchase—all too rare?'

    'Lads of honour! ye, none others,'
Said she, 'are my own, own brothers.

The Dead Princess

If I lie, may God command
That I perish where I stand;
Know ye then, that I am plighted;
What shall serve? I cannot right it.
Ye are equal in mine eyes;
All are valiant, all are wise;
Each one hath my love sincerest;
But another still is dearest;
I must his for ever be;
Elisey, the prince, is he.'

   Mute they stood; and as she ended,
Scratched their necks: 'Be not offended!
Asking, surely, is no sin';
And the eldest bowed: 'We win
Pardon? Is it so?—then say not
In excuse one word.'
                             'I may not
Chide you,' soft the answer came;
'For my *No* I'm not to blame.'
Then they did meet reverence to her;
Quietly retired each wooer;
Lived their old lives, every one,
All in peace and unison.

   But the wicked queen, still fretting,
Not forgiving or forgetting,
On the princess thought, and long
Chafed in anger at the wrong
Done her by the glass, and pouted.
But she threw her arms about it
In the end, and sat her down
Facing it; forgot to frown,

And once more began to preen her;
Said, with smiling gay demeanour,
'Mirror, greetings! Let me hear
Nothing but the truth, my dear;
Tell me, am I sweetest, fairest?
Are my red and white the rarest?'
And the mirror, it replies,
'Thou art lovely, none denies.
Yet in oakwoods green and shady,
All unnoted lives a lady,
Housed with seven champions; now,
She is sweeter far than thou.'
Then the queen in wrath flew at her;
'Thou, Chernavka, in this matter
Durst thou trick me?'—To the rest,
Point by point, the wench confessed.
And that evil queen did warn her
That a collar might adorn her
Set with spikes! 'Now die,' she saith,
'Or the princess do to death.'

Once the young princess, who waited
For her brothers dear belated,
At her window spun; and there
Suddenly below the star
Heard the angry house-dog growling.
There, within the court, was prowling
Just a nun who begged for food
While with crutch the dog she shooed.
Down the lady called, 'Good mother,
I will scare him; stop the pother,
Only wait, and thou wilt see
What I'm bringing down to thee.'
But the nun was heard replying,

The Dead Princess

'Ah, my child, I'm near to dying,
Worried by thy hateful cur;
Watch him, raising all the stir!
Come, come out and help me, darling!'
But the dog, who still was snarling
When the princess tried to go
With a loaf, and stept below,
Pushed between her feet, nor let her
Reach the crone, who moved and met her.
At the crone he still would bay,
And no woodland beast of prey
Could have flown at her more madly.
Was it strange?
     'He's slept so badly!
—Look, and catch!' the princess said,
As she tossed her out the bread.
And the crone, when she had caught it,
Cried her thanks to her who brought it:
'May God bless thee! now, to match,
Here is something for thee: catch!'
And a pippin straight she tosses,
Juicy, fresh, with golden glosses,
To the princess. How the hound
Whimpers, springing from the ground!
—Clap! With both her hands she snatches
And the pippin deftly catches.
—'Say your grace, and eat the prime
Pippin; it will kill the time,
Dearest!' Thus the beldame crying
Bows and vanishes. But flying
With the princess to the stair
Fiercely howls the dog, and there
Sadly looks upon her, making
As his doggish heart were aching

And as though he would command
'Drop the thing!' Her gentle hand
Ruffles, pats him and caresses:
'Falcon, something thee distresses?
Down!' Within her room she passed,
Quietly the door made fast,
By her yarn at window sitting,
Waiting for her hosts; but flitting
Towards her pippin were her eyes.

Ripe and sappy was the prize,
Fresh and fragrant as a posy,
And as golden and as rosy,
As if honey-filled; and she
Through the rind the pips could see.
First she thought that eat she would not
Till the meal; but wait she could not:
To her crimson lips the fruit,
Clasped in either hand, she put.
Nibble upon nibble followed,
And a morsel next she swallowed. . . .

Suddenly the snowy hands
Of our dear one flag; she stands
Reeling, and her breath is stopping,
And the ruddy fruit is dropping,
And she rolls her eyes, and falls
By the ikons on the walls
Headlong to the bench, and by it
Lies, immovable and quiet.

And the brethren, who had made
Some courageous, cunning raid,
Now were trooping homeward proudly.

The Dead Princess

But the house-dog, yelping loudly,
Ran to meet them, showed the way
To the court. 'Bad luck to-day!'
Said the brethren, 'some disaster
Here is certain.' Rushing faster,
Springing in, they looked, and groaned.
And the dog, he barked and moaned,
Fiercely at the pippin flying,
Gulped it down, and tumbled dying,
And expired. Behold, the bait
Was with poison saturate.

Then the brethren bow before her,
In their deepest soul deplore her;
Lift her from the bench, array her
For her burial, but survey her
Wavering—the lady so
Tranquil lay and fresh, as though
Sleep's own plumes were her enwreathing,
And they almost thought her breathing.
So three days they watched; but she
Rose not, slumbering peaceably.
Then the mournful rites they paid her;
In a crystal coffin laid her,
And that young princess in state
All the band conveyed, to wait
On a mountain, named Deserted.
Lofty pillars they inserted
For her coffin, six in all,
At the midnight hour; withal
Safe with iron chains they nailed it;
With a grating round they railed it,
And before their sister dead
Earthward bent; the eldest said:

'*Coffined there, may sleep bestrew thee.*
Swiftly malice quenched and slew thee;
Earth thy beauty still doth gain;
Heaven thy soul must entertain.
Best belovèd we esteemed thee.
Cherished thee, and sweetest deemed thee.
No man had thee for his own;
Thou wert for the grave alone.'

   But the wicked queen was watching
For good news that day, and catching
Secretly her glass, she made
Question as of old, and said,
'Tell me, am I sweetest, fairest?
Are my red and white the rarest?'
In her ear the glass replies,
'Such thou art; and none denies
Thou art sweetest, rosiest, fairest
Of all women, and the rarest.'

   Seeking still his promised bride
Over all the earth must ride
Elisey.   But nought availing
Are his bitter tears and wailing.
He may ask of whom he will,
None to answer has the skill;
In his face they laugh and flout him,
Or they show their backs and scout him.
Then at last the warrior turned
To the Sun, who redly burned:
—'Sun, our luminary, pacing
Yearlong round the skies, and chasing
With warm spring the winter snow,

The Dead Princess

Seeing all men here below,
In the wide world hast thou ever
Seen a young princess? ah, never,
Surely, wilt thou grudge reply:
Her affianced man am I.'
'None, dear youth, have I beholden,'
Said the ruddy sun and golden.
'Is she numbered with the dead?
Yet my neighbour-Moon,' he said,
'Somewhere may have met and faced her,
Or by footprints may have traced her.'

Elisey, whose heart was sick,
Waited till the night fell thick;
Saw the Moon new-risen, and hailed her;
With entreaty thus assailed her:
—'Moon, thou Moon, good friend of mine,
Horned and gilded, who dost shine
In the misty deeps upblazing,
Round of face, and brightly gazing,
Thou whom all the stars survey
Loving still thy wonted way,
In the wide world hast thou ever
Marked a young princess? ah, never,
Surely, wilt thou grudge reply!
Her affianced man am I.'
'Brother,' said the Moon serenely,
'I have marked no maiden queenly.
Only in my turn I dwell
At my post as sentinel.
Doubtless, while she past was flying
I had gone.' And he was crying,
'Ah, the pity of it!' 'Nay,'
Then the clear Moon added, 'stay;

For the Wind will help thee, lover,
And may give thee tidings of her;
Therefore get thee to him now.
So, farewell; and fret not thou.'

   Then he plucked up heart, and speeding
To the Wind, began his pleading:
—'Wind, O Wind, so strong and proud,
Chaser of the flocks of cloud,
Stirrer of the azure ocean,
Ranging space in airy motion,
Going in the fear of none
Saving the Lord God alone,
In the wide world hast thou ever
Marked a young princess? ah, never,
Surely, wilt thou grudge reply;
Her affianced man am I.'

   Said the Storm-Wind: 'Tarry: yonder,
Past where quiet waters wander,
Is a lofty mountain, where
Lies a hole profound; and there
Swings within that hole abysmal,
Chained to pillars, in a dismal
Mirk, a crystal coffin; round
All that barren place are found
No man's tracks; the coffin laden
Is with her, thy plighted maiden.'

   Then the Wind sped on. But he
Gave one sob, and, fain to see
Once again his lady plighted
In her beauty, went, and lighted
On that barren place. Behold,

The Dead Princess

Now a craggy mountain bold
Towers before him, and around it
Lies a barren land to bound it.
Swiftly, swiftly doth he go
To an entry dark below.
There, in blackness melancholy
Swings a crystal coffin slowly;
Crystal-coffined, lies she deep,
His princess, in endless sleep.

   Then with all his might he battered
At his dear one's coffin. Shattered
Suddenly, the coffin broke;
Suddenly the maid awoke;
Looked with wandering eyes around her,
Swayed above the chains that bound her,
Heaved a mighty sigh, and said
'See how long I've laid abed!'

   From the coffin she is creeping;
Ah, for joy they both are weeping!
Now he lifts the maid away
Out of darkness into day
And the two are homeward faring,
Happy, friendly talk are sharing.
Quickly round the tidings ring,
'Saved—the daughter of the king!'

   Idly, that same hour, was waiting
The bad stepdame, and debating
With her glass at home; so ran
Converse, as the queen began:
'Am I not the sweetest, fairest?
Are my red and white the rarest?'

In her ear the glass replies,
'Thou art lovely, none denies,
But the sweetest, rosiest, fairest
Is the princess, and the rarest.'
Up the wicked stepdame leapt,
To the floor the glass she swept
Broken, and rushed out, and straightway
Met the princess in the gateway.
Sick of soul, discomfited
Was that queen, and there fell dead.
Scarce to earth had she been carried,
They made ready to be married.
Then was wedded Elisey
To his bride with no delay.

   Never, since the world's creation,
Saw man such a celebration.
I drank beer, drank mead, and yet
Hardly were my whiskers wet.

THE GOLDEN COCK

Once—in Kingdom Twenty-Seven
—Or the Realm of Thrice Eleven—[1]
Somewhere—reigned a tsar, Dodon,
Terrible and famous, known
From his youth for rashly wronging
All his neighbours. He was longing,
Now that age was creeping close,
To make sure of his repose
And relax from wars and labours.
Now behold, those very neighbours
Harried him, with damage sore
To that aged emperor.

So, to hinder them from raiding
On his frontiers, and invading,
He must needs maintain a host,
Multitudes at every post.
Sleepless, still his captains waited;
Vainly!—they are still belated.
Are they watching southward? no,
From the east comes down the foe.
That amended—see, from ocean
Those untoward guests in motion!
Tsar Dodón can only weep
Tears of rage, and lose his sleep.

What is life, in such conditions
Of disquiet?   He petitions

[1] *Lit.*, 'in the thrice-ninth kingdom, in the thrice-tenth empire'
= 'the other end of Nowhere, fairyland.'

Next for aid an eunuch sage,
Both astrologer and mage.
Couriers fly, and make obeisance;
Soon the wise man is in presence
Of Dodon; and from his poke
Out he pulls a Golden Cock,
Saying, 'Take this fowl, and set him
On a perch aloft; and let him,
This my Golden Cockerel,
Be your trusty sentinel.
He, when all is peace about you,
Shall sit still; but never doubt you
That the moment from afar
Comes the least surmise of war
Or incursion, to beset you,
Mischief unforeknown, to threat you,
Then my Cockerel instantly
Shall perk up his comb on high,
Veering towards the danger, shuffling,
Crowing, and his feathers ruffling.'

   Then his thanks the emperor told
To the eunuch; piles of gold
Proffered, rapt in admiration;
Cried, 'For such an obligation,
Shall the earliest wish of thine
Be fulfilled, as though 'twere mine!'

   So the Cock became the warder,
Perched on high, of every border.
If that faithful watcher e'er
Noted peril anywhere,
He, as though from sleep awaking,
Veered towards it, shuffling, shaking;

The Golden Cock

And '*Kirì-ku-ku!*' he said;
'Rule them, as you lie abed!'
And those neighbours soon were quiet,
Had no heart for war or riot,
When the tsar on every hand
Made so resolute a stand.

   This year flies, and then another.
Cock sits quiet, makes no pother.
But one day a monstrous noise
Tsar Dodon's repose destroys.
'Father of thy people! master!
Rouse thee, sire! behold disaster!'
Thus aloud the captain cries.
Through his yawns the tsar replies:
'Eh, who's there? what is it, say you,
Sirs? and *what* disaster, pray you?'
Says the captain, 'Noise and fear
Fill thy capital; we hear
Once again the Cockerel crowing.'
And the emperor, quickly going
To his window, sees the beast
Flapping, turning to the east.
'Not the time to loiter! hurry,
All to horse! and all men, scurry!'
Off his elder son is sent
Eastward, with an armament.
Then the Cock gives over flapping.
All is peace. The tsar lies napping.

   Eight days pass; but not a word
Of that army has been heard.
Has it fought, or not? No message
Comes unto Dodon. In presage

Yet again the Cockerel crows.
Out a second muster goes,
And the tsar sends forth the other
Son, to aid his elder brother.

Silent is the Cock once more.
Still no tidings; as before,
Eight days pass; and all the nation
Lives them through in consternation.
Now again the crow is heard!
And the tsar conducts a third
Muster eastward, never knowing
What may be the good of going.

Night and day those troops marched on
Till their strength was all but gone;
And the emperor, never sighting
Any camp, or field of fighting,
Or sepulchral barrow, thought,
'How is such a wonder wrought?'

Even with the eighth day's ending
With his host he was ascending
Lofty mountains. In their heart
Stood a silken tent apart
With a magic silence round it.
Near, an army lay; he found it
In a narrow gorge, all dead.
To the tent the monarch sped,
There a dreadful scene descrying:
Both his sons before him lying
Lifeless, mail and helmet gone,
And the weapon of each one

The Golden Cock

Through the other's body. Yonder
In the mead their horses wander
On the trampled turf, and pass
Through the blood-besprinkled grass.

    Then the tsar, with anguish shaken,
Moaned, 'Ah, woe! my children taken,
Both our falcons snared! and I—
It is time for me to die.'
And they all took up his moaning,
And a slow and heavy groaning
Pierced the vales, and quivers went
Through the hills. But swift the tent
Parted wide; and thence, all splendid
As the dawn, a maid descended
—Queen of Shamakhan was she—
Softly to the tsar; and he,
Mute, like owl by sunshine blinded,
Gazed into her eyes, nor minded
In her presence both his sons
Lying dead. But she at once
Smiled on tsar Dodon, and to him
Curtseyed deep, and took and drew him
By the hand, and made him go
Into her own tent; and so
To a table next she led him,
And on many dainties fed him;
Bade him rest, and saw him laid
On a bed of rich brocade.
There, for just a week, beglamoured
And enchanted and enamoured,
Tsar Dodon with her made feast,
Her obedient slave and guest.

Pushkin

Now at last Dodon is speeding
Back, his valiant army leading;
Turns his steps to home again,
With the lady in his train.
Rumour runs before him, crying
Sometimes truth, and often lying.
Near the city gates the throng
By the chariot rush along,
Noisily the empress meeting
And the tsar, who gives his greeting
Unto all; but quickly he
In the crowd a head doth see
Grey as any swan's, and on it
Is a Saracen white bonnet.
'Tis the eunuch, his old friend!

'Ha, good father! heaven send
Health to thee; how now, come nigher;
Tell us, what is thy desire!'
Said the wise man: 'Now at last,
Tsar, our long account we cast.
Mind'st thou, for my service, making
Once a friendly undertaking
That the earliest wish of mine
Should be granted, as 'twere thine?
Give me, then, the lady yonder,
Queen of Shamakhan.'
                    In wonder
Stood the tsar, and thus spoke he:
'Ancient, what hath taken thee?
Some possession of the devil?
Hast thou lost thy wits? what evil
Fancy entereth thy head?
There are bounds, when all is said,

The Golden Cock

Though I made the promise duly.
What to thee are maidens, truly?
Peace, enough. For dost thou know
Who I am? I will bestow
Title of boyar, or treasure,
Or a war-horse, at thy pleasure,
From our stables. Thou canst have
Half my kingdom.'
            'Nought I crave;
Give me nothing but the lady,
Queen of Shamakhan.' So prayed he;
Ever thus the sage replied.

But the tsar, he spat, and cried,
'What, so bold? then nought thou gainest,
Sinner! thus thyself thou painest;
Go, with bones unbroken still;
Drag him hence! it is my will.'

Then the old man fell to wrangling;
But, with certain people, jangling
Pays not; for the sceptre now
Caught him just upon the brow.
Flat he fell, and life departed.
All the city shuddered, started.
Cried the maid, 'Ho ho! He he!
Here's a fearless sinner, see!'
And, though sore perturbed, a tender
Smile the tsar contrived to send her.
Then he rode within the town.

But there came a rustle down,
And the city stared affrighted;
For the Cock flew forth, alighted,

Pushkin

Winging straightway to the car,
On the skull of that great tsar;
Flapped, and gave one peck, and flitted
Upward; and, as earth he quitted,
From the chariot dropt Dodon,
Dying with a single groan.

And, as though that queen had never
Lived, she vanished, and for ever.

Though my story is not true,
'Tis a lesson, lads, to you.

TALE OF THE POPE AND OF HIS WORK-MAN BALDÀ

Porridge-head
Was a pope, who is dead.
He went out a-shopping one day
To look for some wares on the way;
And he came on Baldà, who was there,
Who was going he knew not where,
And who said, 'Why so early abroad, old sire?
And what dost require?'
He replied, 'For a workman I look,
To be stableman, carpenter, cook;
But where to procure
Such a servant?—a cheap one, be sure!'
Says Baldà, 'I will come as thy servant,
I'll be splendid, and punctual, and fervent;
And my pay for the year is—three raps on thy head;
Only, give me boiled wheat when I'm fed.'
Then he pondered, that pope;
Scratched his poll, put his hope
In his luck, in the Russian *Perhaps*.
'There are raps,' he bethought him, '*and* raps.'
And he said to Baldà, 'Let it be so;
There is profit for thee and for me so;
Go and live in my yard,
And see that thou work for me nimbly and hard.'

And he lives with the pope, does Baldà,
And he sleeps on straw pallet; but ah!
He gobbles like four men,
Yet he labours like seven or more men.

Pushkin

The sun is not up, but the work simply races;
The strip is all ploughed, and the nag in the traces;
All is bought and prepared, and the stove is well heated;
And Baldà bakes the egg and he shells it—they eat it;
And the popess heaps praise on Baldà,
And the daughter just pines for Baldà, and is sad;
And the little pope calls him *papa*;
And he boils up the gruel, and dandles the lad.

   But only the pope never blesses
Baldà with his love and caresses,
For he thinks all the while of the reckoning;
Time flies, and the hour of repayment is beckoning!
And scarce can he eat, drink, or sleep, for, alack,
Already he feels on his forehead the crack.
So he makes a clean breast to the popess
And he asks where the last rag of hope is?
Now the woman is keen and quick-witted
And for any old trickery fitted,
And she says, 'I have found us, my master,
A way to escape the disaster:
Some impossible job to Baldà now allot,
And command it be done to the very last jot;
So thy forehead will never be punished, I say,
And thou never shalt pay him, but send him away.'

   Then the heart of the pope is more cheerful
And his looks at Baldà are less fearful,
And he calls him: 'Come here to me, do,
Baldà, my good workman and true!
Now listen: some devils have said
They will pay me a rent every year till I'm dead.
The income is all of the best; but arrears
Have been due from those devils for three mortal years.

The Pope and Baldà

So, when thou hast stuffed thyself full with the wheat,
Collect from those devils my quit-rent, complete.'

It is idle to jar with the pope; so he,
Baldà, goes out and sits by the sea,
And there to twisting a rope he sets
And its further end in the sea he wets.
And an ancient fiend from the sea comes out:
'Baldà, why sneakest thou hereabout?'
—'I mean with the rope the sea to wrinkle
And your cursed race to cramp and crinkle.'
And the ancient then is grieved in mind:
'Oh why, oh why, art thou thus unkind?'
—'Are ye asking *why*? and have not you
Forgotten the time when the rent was due?
But now, you dogs, we shall have our joke,
And you soon will find in your wheel a spoke.'
—'O dear Baldà, let the sea stop wrinkling,
And all the rent is thine in a twinkling.
I will send thee my grandson—wait awhile.'
—'He is easy enough,' thinks Baldà, 'to beguile!'

Then the messenger imp from the ocean darted,
And to mew like a famished kitten started.
'Good morrow, Baldà, my dear muzhik!
Now tell me, what is it, this rent you seek?
We never heard of your rent—that's flat;
Why, we devils have never had worries like that!
Yet take it, no matter!—on this condition,
For such is the judgment of our commission,
So that no grievance hereafter be—
That each of us run right round the sea,
And the quickest shall have the whole of the tax.
Our folk, meanwhile, have made ready their sacks,'

Pushkin

Then said Baldà, and he laughed so slily,
'Is this, my friend, thy device so wily?
Shall the likes of thee in rivalry
Contend with the great Baldà, with *me*?
Art thou the foe who is sent to face me?
My Little Brother shall here replace me.'

Then goes Baldà to the nearest copse;
Two hares he catches, in sack he pops,
And returns to the sea once more,
To the devilkin by the shore.
And he grips one hare by the ear;
'Thou shalt dance to our own balalaika, my dear.
Thou, devilkin, art but young and frail;
Dost thou strive with me? thou wilt only fail;
It is time and labour lost for thee;
Outstrip my brother, and thou shalt see!
So, one, two, three, and away—now race him!'

Then off goes the imp, and the hare to chase him.
And the imp by the seashore coasted,
But the hare to the forest posted.
Now the imp has circled the seas about,
And he flies in panting, his tongue lolls out,
And his snout turns up, and he's thoroughly wet,
With his paw he towels away the sweat,
And he thinks he has settled Baldà. But there!
Baldà is stroking the brother-hare,
And repeating, 'My own, my deary,
Now rest, my poor brother, for thou art weary!'
Then the imp of a heap was struck,
And tamely his tail through his legs he stuck;
At the brother-hare he glanced askew,

The Pope and Baldà

Said, 'Wait, I will fetch the rent for you.'
When he got to his grandad, 'Too bad!' he said;
'Baldà—the young one—got right ahead.'

  Then the ancient fiend had a notion;
But Baldà made a noise and commotion,
And the ocean was vext,
And the waters were parted next,
And the imp slipt out: "'Tis enough, muzhik;
We will send to you all the rent you seek.
But listen; dost thou behold this stick?
Now, choose thou a mark, and take thy pick;
And the one who the stick can farthest shoot, he
Shall have the whole of the rent for booty.
Why dost thou wait? why standest cowed?
Dost thou fear to sprain thy wrist?'—"'Tis a cloud
Up there I await. I will toss thy stick up
Right in the cloud, and will start a kick-up
For you fiends!' And again he had won, had Baldà,
And the terrified imp told his grandpapa.
And Baldà again made the waters roar
And threatened the fiends with the rope once more;
And the imp popped up again; 'Why dost fuss?
If thou wilt, thou shalt have all the rent from us.'

  'Nay, nay,' says Baldà,
'I think it is *my* turn, ha ha!
Little enemy, now the conditions to make,
And to set thee a riddle to crack.
Let us see what thy strength is. Look there
At yonder gray mare:
I dare thee to lift her
And half a mile shift her.

So, carry that mare, and the rent is thine;
But carry her not, and the whole is mine.'
And the poor little imp then and there
Crawled under the mare,
And there he lay lugging her
And there he lay tugging her,
And he hoisted that mare for two paces; but falling
As he took the third, he dropt there sprawling.
Then says Baldà, 'What avails to try,
Thou fool of an imp, with us to vie?
For thou, in thy arms thou couldst not rear her,
But see, between my legs I'll bear her.'
And he mounted the mare, and galloped a mile,
And the dust eddied up; but the imp meanwhile
Ran scared to his grandad, and told him then
How Baldà was the winner again.

 Then the devils, no help for it, rose and went
In a ring, and collected the whole of the rent,
And they loaded a sack
On Baldà, who made off with a kind of a quack.
And the pope when he sees him
Just skips up and flees him
And hides in the rear of his wife
And straddles, in fear of his life.
But Baldà hunts him out on the spot, and see!
Hands over the rent, and demands his fee.

 Then the pope, poor old chap,
Put his pate up.   At Rap
Number One, up he flew
To the ceiling.   At Rap number Two
The pope, the poor wretch,
Lost his tongue and his speech.

The Pope and Baldà

And at Rap number Three he was battered,
And the old fellow's wits, they were shattered.
But Baldà, giving judgment, reproached him: 'Too keen
Upon cheapness, my pope, thou hast been!'

TALE OF THE FISHERMAN AND THE LITTLE FISH

An old man, his old woman with him,
Lived close by the dark blue ocean.
In a shaky mud hut they were living
For just thirty-three years exactly.
The old man with his net would go fishing,
And her yarn the dame would be spinning.
Once he cast his net in the ocean,
And the net came up with mud only.
When he cast out his net the next time
The net came up just with seaweed.
And he cast his net for the third time,
And the net, with a fish it came up,
Not a common fish, but a golden.
Then the golden fish asks for mercy,
Speaking with the voice of a mortal:
'Let me go, old man, into the ocean;
A costly ransom I will give thee;
My ransom is whatever thou wishest.'
The old man marvelled, he was frightened;
Three and thirty years he had been fishing
And never had he heard of a fish talking.
And the golden fish, he released it,
Saying to it a word of kindness:
'Golden fish, now may God be with thee!
For I have no need of thy ransom.
So depart thou into the blue ocean,
A-roaming by thyself in freedom.'

The old man, to his dame returning,
Related to her the mighty marvel:—

The Fisherman and the Little Fish

'I was just a-catching a fish this morning,
Not a common fish, but a golden,
And the fish, she spoke to me in Russian;
She begged to go home to the blue ocean,
And ransomed herself with a costly payment:
I might wish for what I like for ransom!
But I did not dare to take the ransom,
So let her go in the blue ocean.'
The old man from his dame got a rating:
'A simpleton art thou and a blockhead;
Not able to take the fish's ransom!
Why, a trough thou mightst have taken from her;
For ours is all broken and battered.'

Then he went to the dark blue ocean,
And saw the ocean a little ruffled;
And to the golden fish he shouted,
And the fish swam up to him, and asked him,
'What mayst thou be wanting, old fellow?'
The old man answered her, bowing,
'Have pity, O my fish, my princess!
My old woman has rated me soundly;
I am old, she gives me no quiet;
For she is wanting a trough, a new one,
And ours is all broken and battered.'
And the golden fish gave him answer:
'Begone, and grieve not; God be with thee.
For ye shall have your trough, a new one.'

Then back to his dame went the old man.
By the dame was a trough, a new one.
But the dame, she scolds worse than ever:
'A simpleton art thou and a blockhead!
Blockhead, just a trough for thy begging!

Pushkin

There is little *truck* in a *trough*,[1] now !
Get thee back to the fish, thou blockhead;
Bow to her, beg of her a cottage.'

   Then he went to the dark blue ocean
(And the dark blue ocean was troubled)
And to the golden fish he shouted,
And the fish swam up to him, and asked him,
'What mayst thou be wanting, old fellow?'
The old man answered her, bowing:
'Have pity, O my fish, my princess!
For my dame is scolding more than ever;
I am old, she gives me no quiet;
And the old shrew asks for a cottage.'
And the golden fish gave him answer,
'Begone, and grieve not; God be with thee;
Be it so; ye shall have your cottage.'

   He went to his hut; it had been earthen;
But the earthen hut had all vanished.
Before him is a cottage, with attic,
With a chimney all of brick and whitened,
And the gate is made of oaken planking,
The old woman sits there at the window
And mightily she abuses her husband:
'Thou simpleton and perfect blockhead!
Simpleton, thou hast begged a cottage!
Back to the fish, and bow before her;
I would not be a vulgar peasant,
But would be a lady of position.'

   Then he went to the dark blue ocean
(The blue ocean was disquieted)

---

[1] Play, in the original, on *koryto* (trough) and *koryst'* (profit).

The Fisherman and the Little Fish

And to the golden fish he shouted,
And the fish swam up to him, asking,
'What mayst thou be wanting, old fellow?'
The old man answered her, bowing:
'Have pity, O my fish, my princess!
My old woman is fooling worse than ever;
I am old, she gives me no quiet;
She would not be a peasant any longer,
She would be a lady of position.'
And the golden fish gave him answer,
'Begone, and grieve not; God be with thee.'

Then back to his dame went the old man.
What beholds he? a lofty mansion!
On the stairway stands his old woman
In a costly warm coat of sables,
On her crown a brocaded head-dress.
And her neck, with pearls it is loaded;
On her hands are rings, which are golden;
On her feet are shoes, which are crimson.
Diligent servants are before her;
She beats them, she tweaks them by the forelock.
The old man said to his old woman
'Greeting, madam lady and mistress!
Now perhaps thy soul is contented.'
And the old woman squalled out at him
And sent him to the stable to serve there.

So a week goes by, and another.
The old woman is fooling more than ever;
Yet again to the fish she sends him:
'Back to the fish, and bow before her;
I would not be a lady of position;
I want to be a ruler and an empress.'

Pushkin

The old man was in terror, he entreated:
'Old woman, hast thou feasted upon henbane?
How to walk, and how to talk, thou hast forgotten;
Thou wilt set the whole empire laughing.'
The old woman was angrier than ever
And on the cheek she cuffed her husband:
'Peasant, dar'st thou to argue with me,
With me, a lady of position?
Get thee to the sea—and on my honour,
If thou dost not, shalt be taken willy-nilly.'

The old man made off to the ocean
(The blue ocean had darkened over)
And to the golden fish he shouted,
And the fish swam up to him, asking,
'What mayst thou be wanting, old fellow?'
The old man answered her, bowing:
'Have pity, O my fish, my princess!
Again my old woman is rebelling;
Cares no more to be lady of position,
Wants to be a ruler and an empress.'
And the golden fish gave him answer,
'Begone, and grieve not; God be with thee;
Good! thy old woman shall be empress.'

Then back to his dame went the old man.
Lo, before him an imperial palace!
In the palace he sees his old woman
Sitting at the table, an empress;
Her servants are boyars and nobles,
And wine from overseas they pour her;
Gingerbread, all stamped, she is eating.
And a dread bodyguard surrounds her,
They have got axes on their shoulders.

The Fisherman and the Little Fish

When the old man saw them, he was frightened,
Bowed at the feet of the old woman,
Saying, 'I bid thee hail, dread empress!
Now perhaps thy soul is contented.'
The old woman never looked at him,
Just bade them drive him from her presence.
Then ran up the boyars and nobles,
And they scruffed the old fellow forwards,
And up ran the guard at the doorway,
All but chopping him with their axes.
And the common people bemocked him:
'Thou deservest it, thou boorish ancient!
Be instructed, thou boor, hereafter,
Do not sit in the sledges of others!'

So the week goes by, and the next one;
The old woman is fooling more than ever.
She sends her courtiers to her husband,
They hunt out the old man and bring him.
And the dame, she says to her old man:
'Back to the fish, and bow before her;
I would not be ruler and an empress,
I would fain of the sea be sovereign,
So as to live in the sea, the Ocean,
So that the golden fish may serve me,
And go as my messenger on errands.'

And the old man, he durst not oppose her,
Durst not utter a word to cross her.
Now he goes to the dark blue ocean,
He looks—on the sea is a black tempest;
So swollen are the angry billows,
So rush they, such a roar are they raising.
And to the golden fish he shouted,

And the fish swam up to him, asking,
'What mayst thou be wanting, old fellow?'
The old man answered her, bowing,
'Have pity, O my fish, my princess!
How deal with her, my damned old woman?
She wants no longer to be empress,
She wants of the sea to be sovereign,
So as to live in the sea, the Ocean,
That *thou* thyself mayst be her servant
And be her messenger on errands.'
But the fish, not a word she uttered,
She just plashed with her tail in the water
And went off in the depths of ocean.
Long by ocean he awaited an answer
In vain—and went back to his old woman.
See! the old mud hut is before him;
His old woman sits on the threshold,
And before her is a trough in flinders.

'When in the warm springtime'

When in the warm springtime
Out of the white little daybreak,
Out of the forest, the dense forest,
Came the dark-brown Mrs. Bear
With her small bear-cub children
To walk a little, to look a little, to show their faces,
Mrs. Bear sat down under a birch-tree;
The bear-cubs began to play together,
To embrace, to wrestle,
To wrestle, to turn somersaults.

From somewhere or other comes a peasant,
In his hands he carries a boar-spear,
And a knife is there at his belt
And a bag is there on his shoulders.
When Mrs. Bear sighted
The peasant with his boar-spear,
Mrs. Bear set up a roar,
Began to call her little children,
Her silly little bear-cubs:
—'Ah you, little children, you bearlings!
Stop rolling over each other,
Embracing, somersaulting!
Stop, and take shelter behind me,
I will not give you up to the peasant,
I will rip out the peasant's belly!'
The little bear-cubs took fright,
Rushed behind Mrs. Bear.
Mrs. Bear got angry,
Her shag stood up on end.

But that peasant, he was shrewd of wit,
He dashed upon Mrs. Bear,
He planted the boar-spear in her
Above the navel, below the liver.
Mrs. Bear tumbled on the wet earth;
And that peasant, he ript her belly,
Ript her belly and skinned her,
Put the little bear-cubs in the bag,
Put them in and went home.
—'Here, wife, is a present for thee,
A bearskin cloak worth fifty roubles,
And here is another present for thee,
Three bear-cubs worth five roubles each.'

   The noise of this did not go through the town,
It was carried all through the forest,
It was carried to the dark-brown Bear,
How the peasant had killed his Mrs. Bear,
Had ript up her white belly,
Had put the little bear-cubs in a bag.
Then the Bear began to mourn,
Hung his head, roared aloud
For his own dear spouse,
For dark-brown Mrs. Bear:
—'Ah thou, my light, my bear-wife!
For whom hast thou left me,
A widower unhappy,
A widower miserable?
How, my noble lady, shall thou and I
Play our joyous play no more,
Make no more dear children,
Nor rock our little cubs,
Rock them, and lullaby them!'

'When in the warm springtime'

Then the beasts gathered together
To that same Bear, the nobleman:
Up ran the bigger beasts,
Up there ran the lesser beasts.
Up ran Gentleman-Wolf,
His teeth were ready to bite,
His eyes were covetous.
There came the Beaver, trader-guest,
A fat tail had he, the Beaver.
There came Lady Weasel,
There came Princess Squirrel,
There came Mrs. Fox-Secretary,
Mrs. Secretary, Mrs. Treasurer.
There came Mrs. Playful Ermine.
Up ran Rascal-Hare,
Little white Hare, little gray Hare;
There came Marmot the Scoffer;
Marmot, he lives behind the barn.
There came Tapster-Hedgehog:
Hedgehog, ever he curls up,
Ever he puts up his bristles . . .

THE BRONZE HORSEMAN

(A Tale of Petersburg)

'The occurrence related in this tale is based on fact. The details of the flood are taken from the journals of the day. The curious may consult the information collected by V. I. Berkh' (Pushkin's note).

> There, by the billows desolate,
> He stood, with mighty thoughts elate,
> And gazed; but in the distance only
> A sorry skiff on the broad spate
> Of Neva drifted seaward, lonely.
> The moss-grown miry banks with rare
> Hovels were dotted here and there
> Where wretched Finns for shelter crowded;
> The murmuring woodlands had no share
> Of sunshine, all in mist beshrouded.
>   And thus He mused: 'From here, indeed
> Shall we strike terror in the Swede;
> And here a city by our labour
> Founded, shall gall our haughty neighbour;
> "Here cut"—so Nature gives command—
> "Your window [1] through on Europe; stand
> Firm-footed by the sea, unchanging!"
> Ay, ships of every flag shall come
> By waters they had never swum,
> And we shall revel, freely ranging.'

---

[1] 'Algarotti has somewhere said: "Petersbourg est la fenêtre, par laquelle la Russie regarde en Europe"' (*Pushkin's note*).

The Bronze Horseman

A century—and that city young,
Gem of the Northern world, amazing,
From gloomy wood and swamp upsprung,
Had risen, in pride and splendour blazing.
Where once, by that low-lying shore,
In waters never known before
The Finnish fisherman, sole creature,
And left forlorn by stepdame Nature,
Cast ragged nets,—today, along
Those shores, astir with life and motion,
Vast shapely palaces in throng
And towers are seen: from every ocean,
From the world's end, the ships come fast,
To reach the loaded quays at last.
The Neva now is clad in granite
With many a bridge to overspan it;
The islands lie beneath a screen
Of gardens deep in dusky green.
To that young capital is drooping
The crest of Moscow on the ground,
A dowager in purple, stooping
Before an empress newly crowned.
   I love thee, city of Peter's making;
I love thy harmonies austere,
And Neva's sovran waters breaking
Along her banks of granite sheer;
Thy traceried iron gates; thy sparkling,
Yet moonless, meditative gloom
And thy transparent twilight darkling;
And when I write within my room
Or, lampless, read,—then, sunk in slumber,
The empty thoroughfares, past number,
Are piled, stand clear upon the night;
The Admiralty spire is bright;

Nor may the darkness mount, to smother
The golden cloudland of the light,
For soon one dawn succeeds another
With barely half-an-hour of night.
I love thy ruthless winter, lowering
With bitter frost and windless air;
The sledges along Neva scouring;
Girls' cheeks—no rose so bright and fair!
The flash and noise of balls, the chatter;
The bachelor's hour of feasting, too;
The cups that foam and hiss and spatter,
The punch that in the bowl burns blue.
I love the warlike animation
On playing-fields of Mars; to see
The troops of foot and horse in station,
And their superb monotony;
Their ordered, undulating muster;
Flags, tattered on the glorious day;
Those brazen helmets in their lustre
Shot through and riddled in the fray.
I love thee, city of soldiers, blowing
Smoke from thy forts: thy booming gun;
—A Northern empress is bestowing
Upon the royal house a son!
Or when, another battle won,
Proud Russia holds her celebration;
Or when the Neva breaking free
Her dark blue ice bears out to sea
And scents the spring, in exultation.

    Now, city of Peter, stand thou fast,
Foursquare, like Russia; vaunt thy splendour!
The very element shall surrender
And make her peace with thee at last.
Their ancient bondage and their rancours

The Bronze Horseman

The Finnish waves shall bury deep
Nor vex with idle spite that cankers
Our Peter's everlasting sleep!
   There was a dreadful time, we keep
Still freshly on our memories painted;
And you, my friends, shall be acquainted
By me, with all that history:
A grievous record it will be.

I [1]

O'er darkened Petrograd there rolled
November's breath of autumn cold;
And Neva with her boisterous billow
Splashed on her shapely bounding wall
And tossed in restless rise and fall
Like a sick man upon his pillow.
'Twas late, and dark had fallen; the rain
Beat fiercely on the window-pane;
A wind that howled and wailed was blowing.
   'Twas then that young Evgeny came
Home from a party—I am going
To call our hero by that name,

---

[1] 'Mickiewicz, in one of his best poems, *Oleszkiewicz*, has in most beautiful lines described the day preceding the Petersburg flood. It is only a pity that his description is inaccurate. There was no snow—the Neva was not covered with ice. Our description is correct, although it has none of the brilliant colours of the Polish poet' (*Pushkin's note*).—Oleszkiewicz, the painter, mystic, and friend of Mickiewicz, in this poem appears at night in a boat on the Neva, hears the storm rising, and forebodes the flood that is coming on the morrow. He also, under the palace walls, apostrophizes the sleepless Tsar, Alexander I; not, like Pushkin, as a benevolent and sorrowing monarch, but from the Polish standpoint, as one in whose soul the evil principle has prevailed. 'God will shake the steps of the Assyrian throne' (*Translator's note*).

For it sounds pleasing, and moreover
My pen once liked it;—why discover
The needless surname?—True, it may
Have been illustrious in past ages,
—Rung, through tradition, in the pages
Of Karamzin; and yet, today
That name is never recollected,
By Rumour and the World rejected.
Our hero—somewhere—served the State;
He shunned the presence of the great;
Lived in Kolomna; for the fate
Cared not of forbears dead and rotten,
Or antique matters long forgotten.

   So, home Evgeny came, and tossed
His cloak aside; undressed; and sinking
Sleepless upon his bed, was lost
In sundry meditations—thinking
Of what?—How poor he was; how pain
And toil might some day hope to gain
An honoured, free, assured position;
How God, it might be, in addition
Would grant him better brains and pay.
Such idle folk there were, and they,
Lucky and lazy, not too brightly
Gifted, lived easily and lightly;
And he—was only in his second
Year at the desk.   He further reckoned
That still the ugly weather held;
That still the river swelled and swelled;
That almost now from Neva's eddy
The bridges had been moved already;
That from Parasha he must be
Parted for some two days, or three.

And all that night he lay, so dreaming,
And wishing sadly that the gale
Would bate its melancholy screaming
And that the rain would not assail
The glass so fiercely.... But sleep closes
His eyes at last, and he reposes.
  But see, the mists of that rough night
Thin out, and the pale day grows bright;
That dreadful day!—For Neva, leaping
Seaward all night against the blast
Was beaten in the strife at last,
Against the frantic tempest sweeping;
And on her banks at break of day
The people swarmed and crowded, curious,
And revelled in the towering spray
That spattered where the waves were furious.
But the wind driving from the bay
Dammed Neva back, and she receding
Came up, in wrath and riot speeding;
And soon the islands flooded lay.
Madder the weather grew, and ever
Higher upswelled the roaring river
And bubbled like a kettle, and whirled
And like a maddened beast was hurled
Swift on the city.   All things routed
Fled from its path, and all about it
A sudden space was cleared; the flow
Dashed in the cellars down below;
Canals above their borders spouted.
Behold Petropol floating lie
Like Triton in the deep, waist-high!
  A siege! the wicked waves, attacking
Climb thief-like through the windows; backing,
The boats stern-foremost smite the glass;

Trays with their soaking wrappage pass;
And timbers, roofs, and huts all shattered,
The wares of thrifty traders scattered,
And the pale beggar's chattels small,
Bridges swept off beneath the squall,
Coffins from sodden graveyards—all
Swim in the streets!
.... And contemplating
God's wrath, the folk their doom are waiting.
All will be lost; ah, where shall they
Find food and shelter for today?

   The glorious emperor, now departed,
In that grim year was sovereign
Of Russia still. He came, sick-hearted,
Out on his balcony, and in pain
He said: 'No Tsar, with God, is master
Over God's elements!' In thought
He sat, and gazed on the disaster
Sad-eyed, and on the evil wrought;
For now the squares with lakes were studded,
Their torrents broad the streets had flooded,
And now forlorn and islanded
The palace seemed. The emperor said
One word:—and see, along the highways
His generals [1] hurrying, through the byways!
From city's end to end they sped
Through storm and peril, bent on saving
The people, now in panic raving
And drowning in their houses there.

   New-built, high up in Peter's Square
A corner mansion then ascended;
And where its lofty perron ended

---

[1] 'Count Miloradovich and Adjutant-General Benckendorff' (*Pushkin's note*).

The Bronze Horseman

Two sentry lions stood at guard
Like living things, and kept their ward
With paw uplifted. Here, bare-headed,
Pale, rigid, arms across his breast,
Upon the creature's marble crest
Sat poor Evgeny. But he dreaded
Nought for himself; he did not hear
The hungry rollers rising near
And on his very footsoles plashing,
Feel on his face the rainstorm lashing,
Or how the riotous, moaning blast
Had snatcht his hat. His eyes were fast
Fixt on one spot in desperation
Where from the deeps in agitation
The wicked waves like mountains rose,
Where the storm howled, and round were driven
Fragments of wreck. . . . There, God in Heaven!
Hard by the bay should stand, and close,
Alas, too close to the wild water,
A paintless fence, a willow-tree,
And there a frail old house should be
Where dwelt a widow, with a daughter
Parasha—and his dream was she!
His dream—or was it but a vision,
All that he saw? was life also
An idle dream which in derision
Fate sends to mock us here below?
   And he, as though a man enchanted
And on the marble pinned and planted,
Cannot descend, and round him lie
Only the waters. There, on high,
With Neva still beneath him churning,
Unshaken, on Evgeny turning
His back, and with an arm flung wide,

Behold the Image sit, and ride
Upon his brazen horse astride!

II

   But now, with rack and ruin sated
And weary of her insolence
And uproar, Neva, still elated
With her rebellious turbulence,
Stole back, and left her booty stranded
And unregarded. So a bandit
Bursts with his horde upon a village
To smash and slay, destroy and pillage;
Whence yells, and violence, and alarms,
Gritting of teeth, and grievous harms
And wailings; then the evildoers
Rush home; but dreading the pursuers
And sagging with the stolen load
They drop their plunder on the road.
   Meanwhile the water had abated
And pavements now uncovered lay;
And our Evgeny, by dismay
And hope and longing agitated,
Sore-hearted to the river sped.
But still it lay disquieted
And still the wicked waves were seething
In pride of victory, as though
A flame were smouldering below;
And heavily was Neva breathing
Like to a horse besprent with foam
Who gallops from the battle home.
   Evgeny watches, and descrying
By happy chance a boat, goes flying
To hail the ferryman; and he,
Unhired and idle, willingly

Convoys him for a threepence, plying
Through that intimidating sea.
The old tried oarsman long contended
With the wild waters; hour by hour,
Sunk in the trough, the skiff descended
Mid rollers, ready to devour
Rash crew and all—at last contriving
To make the farther shore.
                         Arriving,
Evgeny—evil is his lot!—
Runs to the old familiar spot
Down the old street,—and knows it not.
All, to his horror, is demolished,
Levelled or ruined or abolished.
Houses are twisted all awry,
And some are altogether shattered,
Some shifted by the seas; and scattered
Are bodies, flung as bodies lie
On battlefields. Unthinkingly,
Half-fainting, and excruciated,
Evgeny rushes on, awaited
By destiny with unrevealed
Tidings, as in a letter sealed.
  He scours the suburb; and discerning
The bay, he knows the house is near;
And then stops short; ah, what is here?
Retreating, and again returning,
He looks—advances—looks again.
'Tis there they dwelt, the marks are plain;
There is the willow. Surely yonder
The gate was standing, in the past;
Now, washt away! No house!—O'ercast
With care, behold Evgeny wander
For ever round and round the place,

And talk aloud, and strike his face
With his bare hand. A moment after,
He breaks into a roar of laughter.
　　The vapours of the night came down
Upon the terror-stricken town,
But all the people long debated
The doings of the day, and waited
And could not sleep. The morning light
From pale and weary clouds gleamed bright
On the still capital; no traces
Now of the woes of yesternight!
With royal purple it effaces
The mischief; all things are proceeding
In form and order as of old;
The people are already treading,
Impassive, in their fashion, cold,
Through the cleared thoroughfares, unheeding;
And now official folk forsake
Their last night's refuge, as they make
Their way to duty. Greatly daring,
The huckster now takes heart, unbaring
His cellar, late the prey and sack
Of Neva,—hoping to get back
His heavy loss and wasted labour
Out of the pockets of his neighbour.
The drifted boats from each courtyard
Are carried.　　　　To a certain bard,
A count, a favourite of heaven
To one Khvostov, the theme was given
To chant in his immortal song
How Neva's shores had suffered wrong.
　　But my Evgeny, poor, sick fellow!—
Alas, the tumult in his brain

The Bronze Horseman

Had left him powerless to sustain
Those shocks of terror. For the bellow
Of riotous winds and Neva near
Resounded always in his ear;
A host of hideous thoughts attacked him,
A kind of nightmare rent and racked him,
And on he wandered silently;
And as the week, the month, went by,
Never came home. His habitation,
As time ran out, the landlord took,
And leased the now deserted nook
For a poor poet's occupation.
   Nor ever came Evgeny home
For his belongings; he would roam,
A stranger to the world; his ration
A morsel tendered in compassion
Out of a window; he would tramp
All day, and on the quay would camp
To sleep; his garments, old and fraying,
Were all in tatters and decaying.
And the malicious boys would pelt
The man with stones; and oft he felt
The cabman's whiplash on him flicking;
For he had lost the skill of picking
His footsteps,—deafened, it may be,
By fears that clamoured inwardly.
So, dragging out his days, ill-fated,
He seemed like something miscreated,
No beast, nor yet of human birth,
Neither a denizen of earth
Nor phantom of the dead.
                   Belated
One night, on Neva wharf he slept.
Now summer days toward autumn crept;

A wet and stormy wind was blowing,
And Neva's sullen waters flowing
Plashed on the wharf and muttered there
Complaining—beat the slippery stair
As suitors beat in supplication
Unheeded at a judge's door.
In gloom and rain, amid the roar
Of winds,—a sound of desolation
With cries of watchmen interchanged
Afar, who through the darkness ranged,—
Our poor Evgeny woke; and daunted,
By well-remembered terrors haunted,
He started sharply, rose in haste,
And forth upon his wanderings paced;
—And halted on a sudden, staring
About him silently, and wearing
A look of wild alarm and awe.
Where had he come? for now he saw
The pillars of that lofty dwelling
Where, on the perron sentinelling,
Two lion-figures stand at guard
Like living things, keep watch and ward
With lifted paw. Upright and glooming,
Above the stony barrier looming,
The Image, with an arm flung wide,
Sat on his brazen horse astride.[1]
    And now Evgeny, with a shiver
Of terror, felt his reason clear.
He knew the place, for it was here
The flood had gambolled, here the river
Had surged; here, rioting in their wrath,

[1] 'See description of the monument in Mickiewicz. It is borrowed from Ruban, as Mickiewicz himself observes' (*Pushkin's note*).

The wicked waves had swept a path
And with their tumult had surrounded
Evgeny, lions, square,—and Him
Who, moveless and aloft and dim,
Our city by the sea had founded,
Whose will was Fate. Appalling there
He sat, begirt with mist and air.
What thoughts engrave his brow! what hidden
Power and authority he claims!
What fire in yonder charger flames!
Proud charger, whither art thou ridden,
Where leapest thou? and where, on whom,
Wilt plant thy hoof?—Ah, lord of doom
And potentate, 'twas thus, appearing
Above the void, and in thy hold
A curb of iron, thou sat'st of old
O'er Russia, on her haunches rearing!

   About the Image, at its base,
Poor mad Evgeny circled, straining
His wild gaze upward at the face
That once o'er half the world was reigning.
His eye was dimmed, crampt was his breast,
His brow on the cold grill was pressed,
While through his heart a flame was creeping
And in his veins the blood was leaping.
He halted sullenly beneath
The haughty Image, clenched his teeth
And clasped his hands, as though some devil
Possessed him, some dark power of evil,
And shuddered, whispering angrily,
'Ay, architect, with thy creation
Of marvels. . . . Ah, beware of me!'
And then, in wild precipitation
He fled.

    For now he seemed to see
The awful Emperor, quietly,
With momentary anger burning,
His visage to Evgeny turning!
And rushing through the empty square,
He hears behind him as it were
Thunders that rattle in a chorus,
A gallop ponderous, sonorous,
That shakes the pavement. At full height,
Illumined by the pale moonlight,
With arm outflung, behind him riding
See, the bronze horseman comes, bestriding
The charger, clanging in his flight.
All night the madman flees; no matter
Where he may wander at his will,
Hard on his track with heavy clatter
There the bronze horseman gallops still.
    Thereafter, whensoever straying
Across that square Evgeny went
By chance, his face was still betraying
Disturbance and bewilderment.
As though to ease a heart tormented
His hand upon it he would clap
In haste, put off his shabby cap,
And never raise his eyes demented,
And seek some byway unfrequented.
    A little island lies in view
Along the shore; and here, belated,
Sometimes with nets a fisher-crew
Will moor and cook their long-awaited
And meagre supper. Hither too
Some civil servant, idly floating,
Will come upon a Sunday, boating.
That isle is desolate and bare;

The Bronze Horseman

No blade of grass springs anywhere.
Once the great flood had sported, driving
The frail hut thither.   Long surviving,
It floated on the water there
Like some black bush.   A vessel plying
Bore it, last spring, upon her deck.
They found it empty, all a wreck;
And also, cold and dead and lying
Upon the threshold, they had found
My crazy hero.   In the ground
His poor cold body there they hurried,
And left it to God's mercy, buried.

THE WINTER ROAD

Through the eddying haze and shadows
  Now the moon is making way,
And on melancholy meadows
  Pours a melancholy ray.

Down the wintry road and dreary
  Flies the troika, swift, alone,
And for ever tinks its dreary
  Tiny bell, in monotone;

And the driver's ditty drawling
  Has a homelike sound for me,
Sickness of the heart recalling,
  Or old reckless revelry.

Ah, these snows and wastes, no lonely
  Fire, or blackened hut, beguiles!
But, in slow procession, only
  Motley posts that mark the miles!

—Nina, I return tomorrow,
  And beside thy hearth, dear friend,
Drown my tedium and sorrow,
  Gazing, gazing without end.

While the clock, with ticking finger,
  Circles round, so evenly,
None shall pester us, none linger!
  Midnight parts not thee and me,

The Winter Road

—Nina, sad my way, and weary;
  Mute, the driver nods at last;
Still the small bell tinkles, dreary,
  And the moon is overcast.

TO THE BROWNIE

To thee, our peaceful ground invisibly defending,
   Here is my prayer, O Brownie kind and good:—
   Keep safe my hamlet, and my garden wild, and wood,
And all my cloistered household unpretending!

May never rainstorm hurt these fields with perilous cold;
   May no belated autumn hurricane assail them!
   But helpful, timely snowfall veil them
Above the moist, manuring mould!

By these ancestral shades stay secret sentinel;
   See thou intimidate the midnight robber spying;
   Guard from all ill unfriendly eyeing
The happy cottage where we dwell!

Patrol it watchfully about; thy love betoken
   To my small plot, and stream embankt that drowsy flows,
   And this sequestered kitchen-close
With ancient crumbling wicket-gate and fences broken!

—Love, too, the hillock's slope of green
   And meadows that I tread in idle rumination,
   The cool lime-shades, the maples' murmuring screen:—
These are the haunts of inspiration!

NEKRASOV

THE BIRTHPLACE

Behold it once again, the old familiar place,
Wherein my fathers passed their barren, vacant days!
In muddy revels ran their lives, in witless bragging,
In little bullying ways, in gluttonies unflagging;
The swarm of shivering serfs in their oppression found
An enviable thing the master's meanest hound;
And here to see the light of heaven I was fated,
And here I learned to hate, and bear the thing I hated;
But all my hate I hid within my soul for shame,
And I at seasons too a yokel squire became;
And here it was my soul, untimely spoilt and tainted,
With blessed rest and peace too soon was disacquainted;
Unchildish trouble then, and premature desires,
Lay heavy on my heart, and scorched it with their fires.
The days of a man's youth in memory, 'tis notorious,
Are like a sumptuous dream, are trumpeted as glorious;
—Those beauteous memories file in order before me,
Only to fill my breast with anger and ennui!

Here is the dark, dark close. See, where the branches thicken,
What figure glimpses down the pathway, sad and stricken?
Too well the cause I know, my mother, of thy tears;
Too well I know who marred and wasted all thy years.
For ever doomed to serve a sullen churl untender,
Unto no hopeless hope thy spirit would surrender;

Nekrasov

To no rebellious dream thy timorous heart was stirred;
Thy lot, like any serf's, was borne without a word.
No frigid soul was thine, I know, or void of passion,
But resolute, and framed in proud and lovely fashion;
And all the wrongs that still thy ebbing strength could
    bear
Thy last faint words forgave thy slayer, watching there!
And thou, too, with that sad mute sufferer partaking
Her dreadful lot, and all the outrage and the aching,
Thou also art no more, my heart's own sister, mine!
Out of those doors by cur and servile concubine
Infested, thou must flee from shame unto disaster,
Commit thy lot unto a strange, an unloved master,
Aye, and rehearse afar the doom that fell on her,
Thy mother. Even he, thy executioner,
Shuddered before thy bier, was once betrayed to weeping,
To see thee with that smile so cold and rigid sleeping.

—Now it is blind and blank, that mansion old and gray;
Women and dogs, buffoons and lackeys, where are they?
Gone: but, of old, I know not what oppression leaden
Weighed upon great and small, the weary heart to deaden.
—Unto the nurse I fled. But ah! the nurse! how
    smarted
The tears I wept for her, when all too heavy-hearted!
To hear her name may stir the springs of old emotion,
But long, how long! has been extinct my heart's devotion;
Chance memories arise to trace and trace again
How her insensate love and kindness were my bane;
And lo! my heart again with wrath and rancour swelling!

Nay, from those younger years of harshness and rebelling
No recollection brings one comfortable ray;
But all that from the first ensnared my life, and lay

The Birthplace

Upon me like a ban irrevocably blasting,
All, all began at home, in this my birthplace. Casting
My gaze in loathing round, it gives me comfort still
To see that they have felled the dark pinewood, the chill
Shelter for tired men from summer heats reposing;
The fallows are burnt up, the herds are idly dozing
And hang their heads above the streamlet parched with
    drought;
The crazy mansion, void and sullen, bulges out,
Where once the long dull note of stifled lamentation
Chimed with the clash of cups and shouts of exultation;
Where he who ground the rest beneath him—only he
To live his life, or act, or draw his breath, was free.

TYUCHEV

'The snow still whitens on the lea'

The snow still whitens on the lea,
   But spring is in the noisy streams.
They wake the slumbering banks, and flee;
   They flee with voices and with gleams.

And far and near their voices ring:
   'The spring, the spring is on her way;
We are the messengers of spring,
   Her avant-couriers today!'

The spring, the spring is on her way;
   With choral dance and rosy-bright
The warm and tranquil hours of May
   Haste after her in joyous flight!

ALEXANDER BLOK

'My spirit is old'

My spirit is old; and some black lot awaits me
   On my long road.
Some dream accurst, inveterate, suffocates me
   Still, with its load.

So young—yet hosts of dreadful thoughts appal me,
   Sick and opprest.
Come! and from shadowy phantoms disenthral me,
   Friend unconfest!

—I have no friend but this dim road, far-winding
   Through night and rain;
There, as on some dark sea, no sojourn finding,
   But only pain.

My spirit is old; and some black lot awaits me
   On my long road.
Some dream accurst, inveterate, suffocates me
   Still, with its load.

'Dim grow the edges of the river'

Dim grow the edges of the river;
    Float, onward bound,
Float still, my skiff, without a shiver,
    Whilst I sleep sound.
No monster wave its rest to shatter
    Shall e'er avail,
Though it come moaning down, to batter
    That skiff so frail.
There, in the clean deep vapour yonder,
    My skifflet, float,
Whilst on immortal things I ponder
    In dreams remote.

'*Life*, our bark, has stranded'

Life, our bark, has stranded
   On a shoal profound.
High the shouts of labourers
   Far away resound.
Over the blank river
   Drift alarms, and song.
See, and Someone enters,
   Gray of coat, and strong,
Shifts the timbered rudder,
   Lets the sail go free;
Breasting at the boat-hook,
   Pushes off to sea?
—Quietly the crimson
   Poop wears round at last;
Look, the motley houses
   Now have flitted past!
Far away they're floating
   Gaily; yet, think I,
Us they ne'er shall carry
   With them as they fly!

'Pipes on the bridge'

Pipes on the bridge struck up to play;
Flowers tipt the apple-spray;
And one green star, aloft, away,
Uplifted by an angel, lay.
Miraculous, on the bridge today
To look into the deeps that stay
Aloft, so far away!

The pipe sings loud, the star climbs high.
(Now, shepherd, homeward ply!)
Beneath the bridge the wave sings by:—
'Ah, look, how fast the waters go!
(Forget for ever all thy care)
Thou never saw'st so deep a flow,
So lucid, anywhere . . .
Or listenedst to such deeps below
Of silence, anywhere . . .

Ah, look, how fast the waters go;
When didst thou dream it? Dost thou know?'

'With tears and merriment and pain'

With tears and merriment and pain
My rivulets of rhyme resound
Here at thy feet.
Each rhyme runs fleet
And weaves a living linkèd chain,
Forgetting its own bank and bound.

I see thee through the crystal flow,
And thou art farther than before.
The crystal chants, and weeps; but no,
I cannot shape thy features, so
To bring thee back to me once more
From that far fairyland below.

'Here in the Dusk'

Here in the dusk, as winter fled,
Were she and I—no soul beside.
'Stay, let us watch the moon,' she said,
'Into the rushes plunge and hide.'
But, as a light air floated past,
Rustled the whispering reeds, and went,
Some blue transparent film it sent
Of ice; her spirit was overcast . . .
She's gone; no soul is here beside.
'Tra-la!' so hum I, pacing fast.
Only the moon and reeds at last,
And bitter almond-scent, abide.

'What long-forgotten gleam?'

What long-forgotten gleam is this?
   An instant, through the violinning
   I catch a different strain beginning!
That low, deep voice of hers it is,

—Of her, my friend of old, replying
   To my first love; and I recall
   It always on the days when fall
The snowstorms, blusterously flying;

When traceless melts the past, and when
   'Tis only alien passions tell me,
Tell me a little, now and then,
   Of happiness that once befell me.

RAVENNA

Interred in ages past thou keepest
    All frail and momentary things,
And like a child, Ravenna, sleepest
    Beneath Eternity's drowsed wings.

No slaves, with their mosaics loaded,
    Now pass the Roman gate; and all
The gilding burns away, corroded,
    On the basilica's cold wall.

The rude sepulchral arches weather
    Beneath the ooze's lingering kiss;
O'er coffined queen and monk together
    For ever creeps the verdigris.

Dumb are the burial-halls, and shady
    And chill their doors, lest Galla [1] rise.
The very stones, that sainted lady
    Would calcine with her sombre eyes.

Forgot are wars, wiped out for ever
    Their trail of blood, their harms, their rage.
Placidia, wake not! chant thou never
    The passions of a vanished age!

Far out the sea has ebbed; a riot
    Of roses clasps the wall, in bloom;
The storms of life must not disquiet
    Theodoric, dreaming in his tomb.

[1] Galla Placidia, daughter of Theodosius the Great, died c. A.D. 450.

Ravenna

The people, and the homes they sat in,
    The vine-hung wastes, are graves.   Alone,
The lettered bronze, the sovereign Latin,
    Rings like a trumpet on the stone;

And only the Ravenna lasses
    With mute fixed looks, forbear to hide
A rare, a shy regret that passes,
    For that still unreturning tide.

Sole, nightly o'er those valleys bending,
    The wraith of Dante aquiline [1]
Counts on the Future, to me sending
    His song of the New Life divine.

---

[1] Literally, 'with eagle profile.' The monument of Dante's tomb at Ravenna, which Blok doubtless had in mind, represents the poet in profile, reading. See the reproduction in Paget Toynbee's *Life of Dante*, 1900, p. 132. The *Divine Comedy* was completed at Ravenna. The last line alludes, of course, to the *Vita Nuova*, written much earlier.

ANNA AKHMATOVA

THE WOUNDED CRANE

Even thus, unto the wounded crane
   The rest their trumpet-call repeat,
When, all around, the autumnal plain
   Lies crumbling in the heat.

Pining, I hear their summons loud,
   Their whirr, on wings of gold,
Out of that bank of lowering cloud
   And tangled thicket's hold.

''Tis time that we take wing, take wing
   O'er stream and field today!
For thou hast lost the skill to sing;
Thy hand is all too frail a thing
   To dash thy tears away.'

INDEX

Akhmàtova, Anna, 20, 184
Alexander I, 10, 19, 155 n., 158
Algarotti, Francesco, 152 n.
Andrèev, L. N., 7
Anthology of Russian Lit., Wiener's, 24
Arìna Rodiònovna, 11, 15
Ariosto, Lodovico, 13
Armida, 35

Babarìkha (in *Saltan*), 80 ff.
Baldà, see Pope, *Tale of*
Baring, Hon. Maurice, 9 n., 23 n.
Bayàn, 29
Benckendorff, Genl., 158
Beppo, Byron's, 10
Berkh, V. I., 19, 152
Bessarabia, 10
Birthplace, Nekrasov's, 20, 171–3
Blackwood's Magazine, 22
Blok, Alexander, 8, 20, 175–83
Borìs Godunòv, Pushkin's, 10
Boswell, Prof. A. B., 25
Bronze Horseman (*Mèdny Vsàdnik*), Pushkin's, 8, 10, 12, 18–20, 21, 24, 152–67
Browning, Robert, 20
Bryùsov, V., 18 n., 20 n.
Buyàn (isle; in *Saltan*), 85, etc.
Byron, G. G., Lord, 10, 12, 13

Carlyle, Thomas, 11
Caucasus, 10
Charles XII, 48
Chèkhov, A. P., 7
Chénier, André, 9
Chernàvka (in *Dead Princess*), 112–13, 118
Chernomòr (in *Ruslan*), 31, 36, 40, 42, 44, 47; (in *Saltan*), 94–5, 98, 105, 107
Cossacks, The, Tolstoy's, 8
Crimea, 10

Dante Alighieri, 182
D'Anthès, Baron George, 11
Dead Princess, etc., Tale of, Pushkin's, 16, 109–26
December Revolution (1825), 10
'Dim grow the edges,' Blok's, 176
Divine Comedy, Dante's, 183 n.
Dmìtri Rùdin, Turgenev's, 7
Dodòn (in *Golden Cock*), 127 ff.
Don Juan, Byron's, 10, 13; 'Commander,' 11
Dostoèvsky, T. M., 7
Dryden, John, 7

Elisèy (in *Dead Princess*), 16, 111, 113, 123, 126

185

Index

Evgèny (in *Bronze Horseman*), 155 ff.
Evgèny Onègin, Pushkin's, 10, 12–14, 23, 24, 50–77

Farlàf (in *Ruslan*), 30, 45, 47
Fin (in *Ruslan*), 31, 44, 45, 46
Finns, 152, 153
Fisherman and Little Fish, Tale of, Pushkin's, 17, 142–8
France, French literature, 9, 10, 11

Galla Placidia, 182 n.
Goethe, J. W. von, 50
Gògol, N. V., 7, 15
Golden Cock, Tale of, Pushkin's, 16, 127–34
Goncharòva, Natalie (Pushkin's wife), 11, 17
Guillot (in *Onegin*), 72–4
Gvidòn (in *Saltan*), 85 ff.
Gypsies (Tsygàny), Pushkin's, 10

'Here in the dusk,' Blok's, 180
Hist. of Modern Russian Lit. (to 1881), Mirsky's, 9 n.
Holy Russia, etc., Matheson's, 24

Ingoldsby Legends, Barham's, 17

Jàrintsov, Mme N., 18 n., 24

Karamzìn, N. M., 12, 156
Kashchèy, 28
Khalabàev, K., 9 n.

Khalànsky, M., 12 n.
Khazars, 30
Khvostòv, 162
Kìev, 28, 29, 30, 40, 44, 45, 46, 47
Kitty (in *Anna Karènina*), 8
Kolomna, 156
Konovàlov, Prof. S., 25
Kreutzer Sonata, Tolstoy's, 8

Làrins, the (in *Onegin*), 50, 54, 70
Lel, 29, 30, 64
Lènsky, Vladìmir (in *Onegin*), 50–1, 59, 69, 70–6
Leopardi, Giacomo, 8
Lerner, N. O., 9 n., 16 n., 20 n.
Lèvin (in *Anna Karènina*), 8
'Life, our bark,' Blok's, 177
Life of Dante, Toynbee's, 183 n.
London Mercury, 25
Lost Lectures, Baring's, 23 n.

Marmion, Scott's, 21, 23
Matheson, P. E., 24
Mickièwicz, Adam, 155 n., 164 n.
Mikhàylovskoe, 10, 15, 19
Miloràdovich, Count, 158 n.
Milton, John, 23
Mìrsky, Prince D. S., 9 n., 22
Modern Russian Literature, Mirsky's, 9 n.
Moscow, 9, 10, 11, 77
'My spirit is old,' Blok's, 175

Index

Natàsha (in *War and Peace*), 8
Nekràsov, Nìkolay Alexèevich, 8, 20, 25, 171–3
Neva, river (in *Bronze Horseman*), 152 ff.
News-Letter, 25
Nicholas I, 10, 19
'Nina,' 168–9

Oleszkièwicz, Mickiewicz's, 155 n.
Òlga Làrin (in *Onegin*), 50–1, 52, 59, 69, 70, 76
Outline of Russian Literature, Baring's, 9 n.
Outlines of Eng. Literature Shaw's, 22
Oxford Book of Russian Verse, 9 n.

Pallas, 35
Paràsha (in *Bronze Horseman*), 18, 156, 159
Pares, Sir Bernard, 25
Parny, Évariste, 9
Pechenegs, 45, 46
Peter the Great, 12, 18, 19, 152, 153, 154, 155, 164–6
Phidias, 35
Phœbus, 35
'Pipes on the bridge,' Blok's, 178
Pollen, John, 24
Poltàva, Pushkin's, 11, 12, 19, 48–9
Pope and Baldà, Tale of, Pushkin's, 135–41

Prisoner of the Caucasus, Pushkin's, 10
Prophet (*Proròk*), Pushkin's, (tr. Baring), 23 n.
Pskov, 10
Pùshkin, Alexander Sergèevich, 8–24, 27–151
Pushkin, Mirsky's, 9 n., 22 n.
Pyatigòrsk Circassians, 116

Queen of Spades, Pushkin's, 11

Ratmìr (in *Ruslan*), 30, 40, 45
Ravenna, Blok's, 20, 182–3
Resurrection, Tolstoy's, 8
Rhymes from the Russian, Pollen's, 24
Rìmsky-Korsàkov, 16
Rogdày (in *Ruslan*), 29, 30
Ròzen (in *Poltava*), 48
Ruban, 164 n.
rusàlka (water-sprite), 36
Ruslàn and Lyudmìla, Pushkin's, 10, 11–12, 21, 27–47
Russian Literature, 1881–1925, Mirsky's, 9 n.
Russian Poets and Poems, Mme Jarintsov's, 18 n., 24
Russian Songs and Lyrics, Pollen's, 24
Russians and their Language, Mme Jarintsov's, 24

St. Petersburg, 10, 11, 22, 152; 'Petrograd,' 155; 'Petropol,' 157; 'Leningrad,' 9 n.

Index

Saracens, 116
Schiller, Friedrich, 50
Schlippenbach (in *Poltava*), 48
Scott, Sir Walter, 11, 23
Shakespeare, William, 10
Shamakhàn, queen of (in *Golden Cock*), 131–3
Shaw, T. B., 22
Shelley, P. B., 20
Skàzka, skàzki (*pl.*), 11, 14–18, 24
Slavonic Review, 23 n., 24, 25
Slepchènko, Mr. Basil, 25
Snowstorm, Pushkin's, 11
Solomon, 35
Soskice, Mrs. Juliet M., 20
Spalding, Lt.-Col., 24
Stone Guest, Pushkin's, 11
Struve, Mr. Gleb, 25
Svetlàna, 64
Swedes, 48, 152

Tartars, 116
Tatyàna ('Tànya') Làrin (in *Onegin*), 13, 50, 51–9, 61–9, 70, 76, 77
'The snow still whitens,' Tyuchev's, 174
Theodosius the Great, 182 n.
To the Brownie, Pushkin's, 24, 170
Tolstòy, Count Leo, 8
Tomashèvsky, B., 9 n.
Toynbee, Paget, 183 n.
Translations from Pushkin, Turner's, 24
Trubìtsyn, N. N., 15 n.

Tsar Berendà, Tale of, Zhukovsky's, 15
Tsar Saltàn, etc., *Tale of*, Pushkin's, 15–16, 78–108
Tsargrad (Constantinople), 31
Tsàrskoe Selò, 9, 15
Turgènev, I. S., 7
Turner, C. E., 24
Twelve, The, Blok's, 20
Tyùchev, Fyòdor Ivànovich, 20

Vengèrov, S. A., 9 n.
Vita Nuova, Dante's, 183 n.
Vladìmir (in *Saltan*), 28, 31, 46 n., 47
Voltaire, F. M. A. de, 9

'What long-forgotten gleam,' Blok's, 181
'When in the warm springtime,' Pushkin's, 18, 149–51
Who Lives happily in Russia?, Nekrasov's, 20
Wiener, Dr. Leo, 24
Winter Road, Pushkin's, 24, 168–9
'With tears and merriment,' Blok's, 25, 179
Wounded Crane, Akhmatova's, 24, 184

Yagà, 27

Zarètsky (in *Onegin*), 70, 72–4, 75
Zhukòvsky, Vasìli Andrèevich, 11, 15, 17, 64 n.